GROWING PAINS

Helping Children Deal with Everyday Problems through Reading

Maureen Cuddigan
and
Mary Beth Hanson

American Library Association
Chicago and London 1988

Designed by Kirk Panikis

Composed in Palatino on a
    Quadex typesetting system
    by Point West, Inc.

Printed on 55-pound Glatfelter
    Natural, a pH-neutral stock,
    and bound in 10-point Carolina
    cover stock by Patterson Printing

Library of Congress Cataloging-in-Publication Data

Cuddigan, Maureen.
    Growing pains.

    1. Children—Books and reading.   2. Children's
literature—Bibliography.   3. Child psychology
—Juvenile fiction—Bibliography.   4. Bibliography
—Best books—Children's literature.   I. Hanson,
Mary Beth.   II. Title.
Z1037.9.C8   1988   [PN1009.A1]   011'.62   88-3451
ISBN: 0-8389-0469-6

The paper used in this publication meets the minimum requirements of American National Standard for Information Sciences—Permanence of Paper for Printed Library Materials, ANSI Z39.48-1984. ∞

Printed in the United States of America.

94 93 92 91 90   6 5 4 3 2

For all the children who have touched our lives

Contents

Acknowledgments

Thanks go to Marygail Gilly Parker for her encouragement, valued guidance, and the countless hours she has given to this project from the very start. We are also grateful to Sue Wittsack, Elizabeth Evans, and Tom Lund for their unique contributions. Recognition also goes to the entire staff at the Dakota County Library System and at the Hennepin County Library, Eden Prairie, for helping us obtain books for our bibliography. We are indebted to our loving families for their patience, assistance, and caring, and appreciative of our friends' and coworkers' tolerance. We extend gratitude to Susan Pearson for giving us direction. Special thanks go to Bettina MacAyeal, our editor, for her belief in the value of our work and for her enthusiasm and support in bringing about the publication of this book.

Introduction

People involved with children are beginning to recognize the role that children's literature plays in helping children learn, experience and enjoy life, grow, imagine, and play. As life becomes more complex, children face increasing numbers of traumatic experiences not commonly faced by previous generations. Families move frequently, divorce is common, and exposure to violence is more prevalent. Appropriate literature can help children to cope with current and potential problems and encourage them to develop their own value systems.

In our daily work with children and parents, clients often ask us to recommend children's books that deal specifically with children's concerns. As a children's librarian and a pediatric nurse practitioner, we recognize the need for a resource that can help adults guide and nurture children. This book provides references that adults will find useful in helping children deal with significant life events.

Our professional work has taught us that children's literature can help children learn about and deal with life's experiences. Children's books convey information, yet they also help define feelings and emotions. Although self-help books and bibliotherapy are becoming increasingly popular, we are not therapists, and providing a bibliotherapeutic guide is not our intent. We believe literature has an inherent value, but the selections in our bibliography focus on quality children's books that can help children with the everyday problems they face. These selections are not intended to be a substitute for professional help.

Today's literature acknowledges the cognitive, psychological, and emotional developmental stages of children, and in so doing, adds relevance to their lives. Interesting stories promote understanding, increase sensitivity, and even decrease guilt when a child empathizes or identifies with a sympathetic character. A time of crisis, such as a loss, change, or other stress, can be a time for potential growth if channeled correctly. The acknowledgement and expression of feelings during a crisis can lead to mastery of the experience. Although children might not experience a certain crisis firsthand, it is important for them to learn about problems in society, since understanding and empathizing with other people are part of the socialization of children.

As children journey through these experiences, adults have the unique opportunity to influence the impact a crisis can have on a child. Adults can use books to facilitate and enhance communication with children. However, books are not a replacement for adult/child contact or for everyday life experiences; they are intended to be shared as another dimension in the relationship. Reading together thus can be a time of both learning and nurturing.

Parents and others working with children can achieve the greatest benefit of reading with children if they choose books appropriate for the child's level of development and needs. It is important, therefore, that an adult preview a book before using it with a child. There also are times when children should be prepared for a book's contents. In this case, adults may need to clarify the story for children, or another book may be needed for follow-up. On one occasion, a day-care provider visited the library with her charges and spontaneously selected and read Carol Carrick's book *The Accident* without prior review. The main incident in this book involves a boy seeing his dog get run over by a truck. The result was that all the children were emotionally upset, and many cried. Had the day-care provider known the contents of the book and prepared the children, she might also have chosen to read the sequel *The Foundling* immediately afterward. *The Foundling* describes the grief process of the same boy and his acquisition of a new pet.

Besides a book being used appropriately with a child, we believe it is crucial that it agree with the parents' religious, moral, and philosophical principles. Children between the ages of two through eight are still in the process of developing their own value systems. The use of children's literature provides a wonderful opportunity for caregivers to influence values formation in children.

Perhaps the most important consideration in selecting a good book is that the child and adult enjoy it. The more that parents read to a child, the more that they will understand what is good and works with their particular child. The ability to select good books develops with practice.

Our criteria for selecting books were based on a composite framework of objective and subjective guidelines. We have read and critically judged 2,000 books in order to identify titles for inclusion in this bibliography. *Children's Books in Print* was used to aid in the selection of appropriate titles and to help determine appropriate age levels. Works by recognized authorities Zena Sutherland *(Children & Books)* and Charlotte Huck *(Children's Literature in the Elementary School)* were used to define elements of quality children's literature. Examples of the elements considered include plot, theme, characterization, and illustrations. Only books appropriate in plot and theme were selected for the bibliography. We have not included didactic titles in which the theme overrides the plot. Characters portrayed in the stories are credible. Many of the selections are picture books, and the illustrations are considered worthy of the story. However, because the main focus of our bibliography is the story, the illustrations are not routinely acknowledged.

There may appear to be a tendency to favor the works of certain authors, but each book has been selected on its own merit. Some authors vary greatly in the quality of their writing, while others maintain consistent standards. The writers of each story included seem to be respectful of children and not condescending or didactic in their approach.

Due to the large volume of children's literature (eight children's books are published every day in America), we chose to limit our bibliography. The majority of the books were published between 1976 and 1986, but a few timeless works have also been included. Age range was confined to two through eight years because these are the critical years in a child's development. Unfortunately, few appropriate books are available for toddlers.

The framework for selection was augmented by our educational background and professional experience. Both authors work with children and understand their needs, levels of development, and how they learn. Mary Beth Hanson, a pediatric nurse practitioner for the past 14 years, has cared for thousands of children and encourages the use of children's literature to help patients cope with a variety of problems. Parents and other professionals constantly ask her for recommendations of books to help children affected by problems such as divorce, bedtime fears, and changes in the family constellation. Maureen Cuddigan, a children's librarian for 16 years, has comprehensive experience in the use of children's literature. She routinely recommends to parents and their children books that deal with specific problems. Clients also ask for books written for preschoolers on subjects such as the death of a sibling and sexual stereotyping. Daily, she has the unique experience of observing children as they respond to books.

Highlighting good children's literature is our primary intent. There may be many books available for the subject areas we have defined, but only the best have been chosen for this reference. Despite the abundance of available titles on many subjects, there is a relative dearth of publications in other areas that we felt needed to be addressed. When necessary, we have included small press publications (e.g., American Cancer Society) as well as books that can be considered only moderate in quality. In all instances, we have noted the limitations and our reservations about certain works, but we have also pointed out positive elements in the stories.

Our basic goal in reviewing each book was to select those that can help children better understand themselves and others and that can also help adults understand and empathize with children. No book can be recommended with absolute certainly for any age group or for any child. The final decision rests with the child and with the caregiver.

Guide to Use

The format of the book has been simplified as much as possible despite the variety of topics and number of selections. An introduction to the topic begins each chapter, elaborating on the subject area and suggesting an appropriate use for the books included. The introduction is followed by annotations of the subtopics. Each annotation includes the following bibliographic information: title, author, illustrator, publisher, copyright date, and recommended ages. Books are listed in alphabetical order by title rather than by author, since titles may be more helpful to the novice in the selection process. Unless otherwise indicated, age range denotes interest level, not reading level. Books designated by publishers as beginning readers have been identified and the age level adjusted to six through eight years. The annotation also states whether a book is out of print (O.P.) or not available in traditional format. If books are out of print, they should be available in many libraries. When relevant, a comment on the treatment of the subject, and in some instances on the book's limitations, is noted.

Special features of this resource book include the identification of Caldecott and Newbery Award winners and Reading Rainbow selections in the columns next to the relevant annotations. The identifying symbols are as follows: ©️ for Caldecott Award winners, Ⓝ for Newbery Award winners, and Ⓡ for Reading Rainbow selections. The related titles listed at the end of most chapters are also relevant to the subject covered in a given chapter, but because the focus of those titles better suits a different subject, the annotations appear elsewhere in this bibliography. Additional help can be found in the Author-Title and Subject indexes following the last chapter.

Chapter 1

Behavior

Cheating, Lying, Stealing
Inappropriate Behaviors
Negative Behaviors
Security Blankets

Few children behave in a predictable manner for any length of time. While some may be charming and pleasant virtually all the time, others may be difficult despite skilled and nurturing parents. However, it is more common for children to demonstrate behavior patterns that fluctuate throughout the various stages of development.

At any age, children behave in ways that can arouse mixed responses from the adults in their environment. One adult might perceive a child as defiant, while another adult might respect such conduct as spirited and independent. Despite differences of opinion, society at large often promotes an underlying consensus about certain behaviors. Whereas lying is condemned, for example, truthfulness is valued. Name calling is frowned upon, while kindness is admired.

Children gradually develop a sense of what is acceptable or unacceptable behavior through the influence of caregivers and of society. The translation of this knowledge into specific behavior is closely tied to stages of development and to the child's identification of certain behaviors as successful, whether positive or negative. Much to the bewilderment of parents, some behaviors, such as temper tantrums, may persist because of the response they create.

Certain behaviors seem universal to children at specific ages. Toddlers are prone to temper tantrums when deprived of what they want. Three-year-olds are commonly physically and verbally aggressive, and often wonderful four-year-olds may find that their wild spirits get them into trouble. More complex behaviors are demonstrated by explosive five-year-olds, who try to be truthful but are not always successful. Six-year-olds are not naughty just to be bad, but fight to be first, and these delightful children may lie and steal. Seven-year-olds show further sophistication of negative behaviors with their complaining, as do eight-year-olds, with their cheating and oppositional traits.

The natural progression of behaviors common at different ages is further influenced by the development of conscience. The ability to evaluate right and wrong is achieved as children move away from egocentrism,

1

not only with time, but also through contact with others in their environment. The dawning of free choice is complicated by temptation and guilt. Late preschool and early school-ages children demonstrate primitive signs of internal government but are easily swayed. Rule-breaking behavior is primarily undertaken to outwit adults. By age seven or eight, a child's conscience is less externally based and allows him or her more freedom to decide between positive or negative behavior.

The need to internalize limits is observed in the youngest toddler. The ability to have self-control and internal regulation provides a sense of security to children and contributes to good self-esteem. To be successful in life, children need to be adaptable and to function in a flexible way. They must learn to work through frustrations, gain skills in cooperative action, and find acceptable ways to fulfill their needs while respecting others. For instance, Andrew Otter, a character in the book *Honest Andrew*, struggles with the fine line between truth and tact, depicting the intricacies of adjusting behavior to meet a situation in a socially acceptable manner.

A crucial factor in achieving pro-social behavior is the degree of involvement of parents and other caregivers. Children receive this help through daily association with loving adults who understand their needs and respect their individuality within the confines of society's demands. The incredible responsibility adults have in molding a child's actions can be eased by understanding child development, and factors that affect behavior, and by scrutinizing one's own value system. Aided by these guidelines, caregivers can set limits and direct children's urges in order to promote behavior that is acceptable to one's family and community.

Children adapt their behaviors and develop their own standards within the context of these rules and role modeling. Good examples of positive behavior patterns can be an invaluable asset in teaching appropriate behaviors. Adults can provide children with these experiences through their own responses and with the help of characters readily available on television and in literature.

Television programs and printed material can expose children either to crime and a meaningless life or to pro-social behavior and a sense of fulfillment. One can choose either to blunt one's moral values or to increase one's sense of personal responsibility. While television is generally accessible, it is often a solitary experience. Books offer parents a unique advantage when caring for children.

Books shared between children and their caregivers promote closeness and affection through purposeful communication. Carefully selected stories can facilitate discussion that reinforces the adult's value system. Books that respect children's integrity can demonstrate limits without being intrusive, controlling, or didactic. Stories can help children understand that other people have problems and experiences similar to their own. Reading can help children experience life vicariously.

Identification with a realistic character moves children beyond their egocentrism and toward an understanding of what is appropriate behavior. The words and actions of characters and the role models they provide help teach acceptable limits. Children can recognize boundaries against which they can test their own ideas.

Stories about eating problems and refusing to go to bed or to bathe are not included in this chapter. Books about not wanting to go to bed usually deal with nighttime fears and therefore are included in the chapter on fears. Eating and bathing problems are usually too superficially treated in the books available on those topics. Only the best books available to help children and caregivers focus on behavioral concerns are included in this chapter.

Cheating, Lying, Stealing

A Big Fat Enormous Lie, Marjorie W. Sharmat, Ill. by David McPhail, Dutton, 1978. Ages 4–7.

The narrator lies to his father about eating some cookies. He regrets his untruth and envisions the lie as an enormous, fat, runny-nosed monster. However, none of the boy's insults will drive Lie away. Finally, imagining that the monster is sitting on him, the boy agrees to tell the truth. Hilarious illustrations.

Dinner Ladies Don't Count, Bernard Ashley, Ill. by Janet Duchesne, Watts, 1980. O.P. Ages 7–10.

Arriving at school in a foul mood, Jason purposely destroys his classmate's model. Unjustly accused of taking the same child's birthday cards, Jason finally reveals to a dinner lady (a school staff person) his disappointment over not being able to get a dog for his own birthday. Empathizing, she helps Jason to accept responsibility for his own behavior and to find the missing cards. British colloquialisms.

Honest Andrew, Gloria Skurzynski, Ill. by David Wiesner, Harcourt, 1980. Ages 6–8. A Let-me-read book.

Andrew Otter gets into trouble for not admitting his dislike of crayfish. Enjoined by his father to always be honest, Andrew is, with devastating results. After insulting several neighbors with his veracity, Andrew and his father have another talk. For children struggling with the fine line between truth and tact.

I'll Tell on You, Joan Lexau, Ill. by Gail Ownes, Dutton, 1976. O.P. Ages 6–9.

Friends Mark and Rose try out for a baseball team coached by a man with a reputation for prejudice against girls. When Mark's dog bites the coach's daughter, Rose urges Mark to tell, but he refuses. After two days of agonizing and strained friendship, Mark finally confesses. Both are surprised to make the team.

Ivan the Great, Isabel L. Cusack, Ill. by Carol Nicklaus, Crowell, 1978. O.P. Ages 7–9.

Only Robby can hear and understand his new parrot, Ivan. After a girl takes his lunch box and other children bully him, Robby is accused by his parents of lying. Since no one believes him anyway, Robby does start lying. In a humorous conclusion, Ivan helps a confused Robby distinguish between truth and falsehood.

Liar, Liar, Pants on Fire!, Miriam Cohen, Ill. by Lillian Hoban, Greenwillow, 1985. Ages 5–7.

The new first grader, Alex, claims to have better possessions than the other children. When his claim proves false, his classmates brand Alex a liar. Despite the teacher's plea for understanding, Alex is ostracized until the Christmas party. His admission of untruthfulness finally garners him acceptance.

Molly's Lies, Kay Chorao, Clarion, 1979. O.P. Ages 4–8.

Molly's penchant for lying results in her new classmates' distrust and a lack of friends. Then Molly helps a boy who's fearful of heights and in so doing makes a friend. From him she learns that telling the truth, painful as it is, can have benefits.

Shnook the Peddler, Maxine Schur, Ill. by Dale Redpath, Dillon, 1985. Ages 7–10.

While Shnook, a visiting peddler, packs up, Leibush, a young Russian Jew, pockets a beautiful dreidel (toy), thinking the foolish peddler will never miss it. Later, a remorseful Leibush seeks Shnook, who welcomes him. The peddler is aware of the theft, but explains that Leibush's anger with himself is sufficient punishment. *Highly recommended*.

The Sign in Mendel's Window, Mildred Phillips, Ill. by Margot Zemach, Macmillan, 1985. Ages 5–8.

Poor butcher Mendel and his wife, Molly, rent half their shop to a man called Tinker. The conniving Tinker claims he wants the space only to think, but he plans to trick the guileless Mendel out of his money. When Tinker accuses Mendel of stealing, Molly and the townspeople expose Tinker as the real thief.

The Three Friends, Susanne Kubler, Macmillan, 1984. Ages 5–8.

Duffel Bear and Sam Hare are enthralled with the adventure stories of their friend Cat, but other animals warn that Cat is a liar. Ashamed, Cat flees, leaving Duffel and Sam lonely. They find Cat and discover a way for him to continue his wonderful storytelling in an honest way.

The True Francine, Marc Brown, Little, 1981. Ages 5–8.

When her best friend, Muffy, cheats at school, Francine is blamed and must stay after school all week. Francine stoically misses softball practice and ignores Muffy. Overcome by guilt, Muffy confesses when their class team is losing. Francine hits the winning run and forgives Muffy. Delightful animal characters overcome the blatant message.

Wishful Lying, Rose Blue, Ill. by Laura Hartman, Human Sci. Pr., 1980. Ages 5–10.

Jody's mother is sick, and his father works long hours. Jody concocts lies to allay his fears that they don't love him. When his lying causes difficulties at school, Jody and his parents painfully examine their behavior and try to make changes. Obviously a "problem" book, but with a sensitive treatment of the subject.

Inappropriate Behaviors

Cloud over Clarence, Marc Brown, Dutton, 1979. O.P. Ages 4–7.

Clarence Cat's life is riddled with accidents because he's inattentive and forgetful. After he rides into a tree and dumps ice cream on someone's head, Clarence's friends present him with a scroll urging him to think about what he is doing. The cloud over Clarence's head finally is lifted.

Duncan and Dolores, Barbara Samuels, Bradbury Pr., 1986. Ages 5–8.

Dolores lavishes attention on her new cat, Duncan. Despite her sister Faye's warnings, Dolores tries dressing Duncan in doll clothes and making him perform tricks. Despairing when Duncan prefers Faye, Dolores begins ignoring him. She quietly rejoices when this behavior wins Duncan's favor, but suffers a setback by reverting to her former exuberance.

Fearless Leroy, Osmond Molarsky, Ill. by Robert Bartram, McKay, 1977. O.P. Ages 7–9.

No one believes Leroy, the new kid, when he claims that his father is "Fearless Fantini," daredevil circus performer. Leroy tries to prove he's fearless, too. His new friends' admiration changes to concern as Leroy's stunts become increasingly reckless. Reunited with his father, Leroy finally admits his fears and chooses safer activities.

The How: Making the Best of a Mistake, Selma Boyd and Pauline Boyd, Ill. by Peggy Luks, Human Sci. Pr., 1981. Ages 4–8.

The narrator becomes flustered when asked a question at school and answers that cows give milk and eggs. His classmates' teasing compounds his embarrassment, and he can barely control his anger. After making a "how" (cow and hen) from clay, the boy experiences the satisfaction of his classmates laughing with him instead of at him.

I Want That!, Anne S. O'Brien, Holt, 1985. Ages 2–3½.

Meagan pulls a doll away from Nicholas. His crying upsets her, so she offers to share the doll. Playing together, they have much more fun. A board book to introduce the concept of sharing.

Oliver Hyde's Dishcloth Concert, Richard Kennedy, Ill. by Robert A. Parker, Little, 1977. O.P. Ages 6–8.

Oliver becomes a recluse when his wife dies. He covers his face with a dishcloth and won't speak. When the cantankerous Oliver agrees to fiddle at a wedding if everyone wears dishcloths over their heads, mischance allows him to experience the harshness his wall of silence has imposed on others. He then invites everyone to dance joyfully.

That's Mine!, Elizabeth Winthrop, Ill. by Emily McCully, Holiday, 1977. O.P. Ages 3–6.

A sister and brother argue over who is building the bigger block tower. Their competition ends with each knocking down the other's effort. With their blocks all mixed up, they decide to build a castle together. Their combined work produces a magnificent structure in which they play happily.

Wheels, Jane R. Thomas, Ill. by Emily A. McCully, Clarion, 1986. Ages 4–7.

Elliot is thrilled with his new bike from Grandpa. Now he can win the Saturday races at the park. But despite all of his determination and fast pedalling, he only ties for last place. Elliot stomps off to pout until Grandpa helps him understand the real meaning of being a winner.

The Year of Mr. Nobody, Cynthia King, Ill. by Malcolm Carrick, Harper, 1978. O.P. Ages 6–9.

Abbot creates imaginary Mr. Nobody when size and age thwart his participation in his brother's activities. Mr. Nobody does wonderful things, such as providing an illusionary knife when Abbot wants a jackknife. Faced with danger, Abbott realizes that pretending won't help him because only a real person can perform a brave act. *Highly recommended.*

Negative Behaviors

Anyhow, I'm Glad I Tried, Judith Vigna, Whitman, 1978. O.P. Ages 5–7.
Irma Jane is downright nasty to her classmate, the narrator. Although the narrator despises Irma Jane, her mother encourages the narrator to be nice. Irma Jane accepts a birthday cake baked by the narrator's mother but is hostile. Exasperated, the narrator leaves, never realizing the joy the cake brings to the mistrusting Irma Jane.

Bubba and Babba: Based on a Russian Folktale, Maria Polushkin, Ill. by Diane De Groat, Crown, 1976. Ages 5–8.
Lazy bears Bubba and Babba constantly argue about household chores. One night they leave the dinner dishes, agreeing that the first one up will wash them. Spending the next day in bed, they arise simultaneously to investigate strange sounds. They find Raccoon cleaning up their mess and admit their foolishness.

The Case of the Stolen Bagels, Hila Colman, Ill. by Pat G. Porter, Crown, 1977. O.P. Ages 7–9.
Paul's reputation as a troublemaker and his love of bagels prompt his teacher's accusation that he destroyed some bagels intended for a class project. He realizes the consequence of his past offenses. Through clever detective work, Paul reveals the culprit, restores his honor, and changes his negative attitude about school.

Don't Be Mad, Ivy, Christine McDonnel, Ill. by Diane De Groat, Dial, 1987. Ages 6–10.
Six funny episodes about Ivy's temptations and triumphs. Ivy wants to keep the bulldozer she bought for Bill's birthday. Later she nearly blames Leo for both of their misbehavior. She suffers qualms when "borrowing" Phyllis' toy bear without asking. However, Ivy's sense of fairness ultimately helps her behave honorably toward her friends.

Don't Touch!, Suzy Kline, Ill. by Dora Leder, Whitman, 1985. Ages 3–7.
Dad and Mom warn Dan not to touch the hot pan and wet paint. Dan continually hears "Don't Touch" from grandparents, siblings, and others. Dejected, Dan takes out his clay and touches, squeezes, and pokes it. Frustrations relieved, Dan produces a model on which he posts the sign, "Don't Touch."

Fox and His Friends, Edward Marshall, Ill. by James Marshall, Dial, 1982. Ages 6–8. Dial easy-to-read.
Three humorous stories about how responsibilities interfere when Fox would rather play with his friends. In two stories, Fox must care for his younger sister Louise, who challenges his authority. In the third story,

Fox deserts his post as a traffic patroller to go swimming, but rushes back when reminded of his shirked duties.

Herbie's Troubles, Carol Chapman, Ill. by Kelly Oechsil, Dutton, 1981. Ages 5–7.

Schoolmate Jimmy John ties Herbie's jacket in knots, ruins his painting, and smashes his granola bar. Herbie's friends suggest ways of ending the torture, but neither sharing nor fighting work. Herbie himself successfully stops the bully by ignoring him. Jimmy John declares that tormenting Herbie is not fun anymore.

Horrible Hannah, Barbara Bottner, Ill. by Joan Drescher, Crown, 1980. O.P. Ages 5–8.

After seeing the warning on the new neighbor's lawn about "Horrible Hannah," sisters Toby and Lucy don't give the new girl a chance. They decide to be nasty to her before she can be horrible to them. Then the sisters discover that the warning involves a sick dog. Toby and Lucy make amends and offer the girl friendship.

I Can Share, Karen Erickson, Ill. by Maureen Roffey, Scholastic, 1985. Ages $2^1/2$–5.

The young narrator is possessive of his toys and refuses to share them with another child. When he tells her to leave, his father explains that sharing does not mean giving his toys away. The boy learns the give-and-take of sharing and the joy of having a playmate.

If He's My Brother, Barbara Williams, Ill. by Tomie de Paola, Harvey House, 1976. Ages 3–6.

A young boy questions why he cannot do whatever he wants to with the things he considers his belongings. He fantasizes about putting worms in his pockets, jumping on his bed, and walking on the roof. His final fantasy concerning punching his brother shows the consequences of his behavior when the brother retaliates.

Kate's Box, Kay Chorao, Dutton, 1982. Ages 3–5.

When Kate hears that cousin Otto is coming, she hides in a box. She jealously remembers the attention previously bestowed on Otto. Today, however, nothing pleases Otto, so he howls and howls. When everyone deserts them, Kate puts the box over Otto and makes him laugh. Discovering an affinity, the two contentedly doze.

Marcella's Guardian Angel, Evaline Ness, Holiday, 1979. Ages 6–8.

Marcella cannot get rid of her newly arrived guardian angel. Angel chides Marcella whenever she is naughty. Eventually, Angel agrees to leave if Marcella will play the Flip-Flop game wherein every negative behavior is replaced by a positive one. Marcella learns the benefits of her developing conscience brought to life through Angel.

Mean Maxine, Barbara Bottner, Pantheon, 1980. Ages 4–8.

Maxine torments Ralph by calling him names. His brother suggests that Ralph stand up to her. This suggestion shocks Ralph, but after some consideration, Ralph fantasizes himself in the guise of different monsters overwhelming Maxine. When the real showdown comes, Maxine is impressed and asks Ralph to show her how he transforms himself.

Move Over, Twerp, Martha Alexander, Dial, 1981. Ages 5–6.

Jeffrey is thrilled to start taking the school bus. However, his excitement is marred when an older kid keeps claiming Jeffrey's seat and calling him "Twerp." When his family's advice fails, Jeffrey puts a "Supertwerp" design on his shirt. Jeffrey's humor earns him back the seat and the older child's respect.

No Boys Allowed, Susan Terris, Ill. by Richard Cuffari, Doubleday, 1976. O.P. Ages 7–9.

Having four older sisters, Tad often feels he needs "boys' lib." Rebelling on his mother's birthday, he takes the bus downtown to buy her a gift but forgets to save enough money for return fare. After spending all of his money, Tad has a frightening two-hour walk home. He emerges triumphant and independent.

Pippin and Pod, Michelle Cartlidge, Pantheon, 1978. O.P. Ages 3–5.

Young mice Pippin and Pod behave mischievously as they shop with their mother. Then they sneak off to cause more trouble. At the pond, they are accosted by bullies. Frightened, Pippin and Pod run away but realize they are lost. Mother finds her children and is angry, but she is relieved to have them back.

Russell Rides Again, Johanna Hurwitz, Ill. by Lillian Hoban, Morrow, 1985. Ages 6–8.

Six delightful stories about irrepressible Russell. In one story, scorning play with his sister, Russell teaches her to count. Another time, Russell is ungrateful at his sixth birthday party until his sense of humor helps him make amends. In yet another tale, riding his new bicycle almost defeats Russell, but he accidentally masters it.

Sam's Car, Barbro Lindgren, Ill. by Eva Eriksson, Morrow, 1982. Ages 2–4.

Sam is happily playing with his car when Lisa comes to visit. When he won't let her play with it, Lisa hits him. Sam retaliates, and both end up in tears until Mother brings them another car. A simple introduction to the concept of sharing.

Sara and the Pinch, Carla Stevens, Ill. by John Wallner, Houghton, 1980. Ages 5–8.

Sara's obnoxious behavior causes problems in three stories. Sara leaves her boots on the bus, pinches classmates, and is rude on her birthday. Mr. Zamatsky, the school custodian, lends Sara his boots and gives her clay to pinch. In return, Sara willingly sacrifices her own birthday cupcake for Mr. Zamatsky.

So What If I'm a Sore Loser?, Barbara Williams, Ill. by Linda S. Edwards, Harcourt, 1981. Ages 5–8.
   Maurice lives in a grand apartment and plays drums. His cousin Blake lives in a dilapidated apartment and hums. During visits to Maurice, Blake is constantly outmaneuvered, then called a "sore loser." Blake finally plays host and proves his winning ability, but then arrogant Maurice accuses him of being a "sore winner."

The Thinking Place, Barbara M. Joosse, Ill. by Kay Chorao, Knopf, 1982. O.P. Ages 4–7.
   Elisabeth is sent to "the thinking place" to ponder her misdoing of putting candy corn in the dishwasher. In the quiet isolation, Elisabeth imagines fictitious Melissa bringing her treats and then a monster frightening her. The solitude gives Elisabeth a chance to consider future atrocities and how to prevent temptations. Illustrations vividly depict Elisabeth's feelings.

Wendy and the Bullies, Nancy K. Robinson, Ill. by Ingrid Fetz, Hastings, 1980. Ages 7–9.
   Wendy is plagued by bullies, and her parents cannot help her. When her best friend gets sick, Wendy must face the bullies alone. Both faking an illness and standing up to her chief tormentor fail. When her dog is harrassed by a bully, Wendy finally successfully fights back. She becomes a leader with new friendships and no bullies.

Wild Robin, Susan Jeffers, Dutton, 1976. Ages 5–8.
   Wild Robin doesn't like doing chores. His sister Janet often pities him and helps out. When Robin is kidnapped by fairies, he may do whatever he pleases. Hedonism soon palls, and a kindly elf shows Janet how to rescue her wayward brother. The book's fairytale style makes a strong message about misbehavior palatable.

Wretched Rachel, Diane Paterson, Dial, 1978. O.P. Ages 3–6.
   Sometimes Rachel is downright wretched. She is naughty to her parents and nasty to her brother, sister, and friends. At other times, Rachel is truly wonderful. Despite the variability of Rachel's behavior, everyone loves her. A humorous depiction of a spirited child.

Security Blankets

The Blanket That Had to Go, Nancy E. Cooney, Ill. by Diane Dawson, Putnam, 1981. Ages 4–6.

Susi's blue blanket goes everywhere with her; it's both a plaything and a friend. With kindergarten starting soon, Susi is told that she cannot take the blanket with her to school. Desolate at first, she works hard to prevent the impending deprivation and cleverly manages to take part of her old friend to school.

Bye-Bye, Old Buddy, Deborah Robison, Clarion, 1983. Ages 5–7.

Jenny loves her baby blanket. It has always been a comfort to her, but now her attachment is causing trouble. Jenny searches for a parting that is neither sad nor embarrassing, and she finally makes the blanket an anonymous gift. The recipient is delighted to share it with his kittens.

Geraldine's Blanket, Holly Keller, Greenwillow, 1984. Ages 2½–6.

Geraldine Pig takes her pink baby blanket everywhere. As Geraldine grows bigger and the blanket gets worn, her parents encourage her to put it aside. Geraldine refuses, even though they insist that she give up the blanket when she gets a new doll. Clever Geraldine makes her blanket into a doll's dress.

The Prince and the Pink Blanket, Barbara Brenner, Ill. by Nola Langner, Four Winds Pr., 1980. O.P. Ages 4–7.

Hal adores his tattered pink blanket, but his father, the king, despises it. The king forbids children to carry blankets, and the prince becomes distraught. However, a wizard reveals that the king once had a special blanket. A new proclamation is issued for the children once the king realizes that some famous people have had security blankets.

Related Titles

Inappropriate Behaviors

Hound and Bear, Dick Gackenbach.

Negative Behaviors

Don't Forget to Come Back, Robie H. Harris.

Even If I Did Do Something Awful, Barbara Hazen.

I'm Terrific, Marjorie W. Sharmat.

May I Visit?, Charlotte Zolotow.

Nadia the Willful, Sue Alexander.

A Weekend with Wendell, Kevin Henkes.

Chapter 2

Child Abuse and Neglect

Informational
Problem-Related
Strangers

The maltreatment of children dates back to the beginning of civilization and remains with us today. Despite the current epidemic of child abuse, neglect, and abduction, prior to 1980 there was an absence of books written for children between the ages of 2 and 8. Throughout the years, parents have given their children vague warnings to beware of strangers. Statistics now demonstrate that mere warnings are not sufficient.

In 1984, 1,727,000 cases of physical abuse, neglect, and sexual abuse were reported in the United States. Of the 200,000 cases of sexual abuse, 100,000 instances were substantiated and intervention services offered. However, these overwhelming statistics do not account for most neglect and other abuse cases, which continue to go unreported and unaided. Such information causes parents and other caretakers to react in panic while they seek ways to protect their children.

Rather than transmit their fear to children, adults can use books to foster communication and teach children about abuse and abduction while helping children increase their self-reliance. Today's literature can help educate children about potential dangers and teach them the benefits of avoiding strangers, following safety rules, having a sense of privacy about one's body, and knowing that not all adults can be trusted. Books also help parents discuss these topics comfortably with children and in a way that reduces embarrassment. Parents need to ensure the safety of their children, and the surest protection is education.

Children are totally dependent on parents and other adults to meet their needs. They have the right to secure, nurturing surroundings. Loving adults can help meet their responsibility by sharing books on these sensitive topics with children.

There are a limited number of books available on these subjects. Of those available, many tend to be simplistic or didactic. The books with reservations have been included in this chapter because of their redeeming qualities.

Informational

A Better Safe Than Sorry Book: A Family Guide to Sexual Assault Prevention, Sol and Judith Gordon, Ill. by Vivien Cohen, Ed-U Pr., 1984. Ages 3–8.

The loving care of trusted adults and the joys of childhood are emphasized in this informational book. Children are encouraged to demand respect for their bodies and, if violated, to tell a trusted adult. The parents' guide provides facts and underscores the importance of being an "askable" adult. *Highly recommended*.

Do You Have a Secret?, Pamela Russell and Beth Stone, Ill. by Mary McKee, CompCare Pub., 1986. Ages 4–8.

There are happy secrets of childhood, but others are frightening. In this nonfiction book, children are encouraged to tell someone if they bear the secret of sexual abuse. They are reassured of their self-worth and given suggestions on whom to tell. Helpful introduction to a sensitive topic. Adult guide included.

Help Yourself to Safety: A Guide to Avoiding Dangerous Situations with Strangers and Friends, Kate Hubbard and Evelyn Berlin, Ill. by Marina Megale, Franklin, 1985. Ages 5–9.

A nonfiction book beginning with the premise that as children grow, they must learn how to keep themselves safe. Seven children are shown avoiding potentially dangerous situations. Scenarios include: a lost child, a possible abduction, and how to find a safe route to school. Safety tips for children and adults are given.

It's My Body, Lory Freeman, Ill. by Carol Deach, Parenting Pr., 1982. Ages 3–6.

An excellent introductory book for the preschool child on how to recognize, avoid, and resist unwanted touching. The child's rights over his or her body and feelings are acknowledged, and a means of expressing these are given. Parents are encouraged to practice the touching codes demonstrated here.

It's Okay to Say No!, Robin Lenett with Bob Crane, Ill. by Frank C. Smith, Tom Doherty, 1985. Ages 4–8.

A parent-child manual for the protection of children. The parent section offers information on child molesters, advice on the workings of a child's mind, and tips on practicing how children should handle dangerous situations. The children's section depicts numerous situations in which children can protect themselves from victimization.

My Body Is Private, Linda W. Girard, Ill. by Rodney Pate, Albert Whitman, 1984. Ages 5–9.

Julie talks about the meaning of privacy and how it relates to one's own body. Some forms of touching are described as warm and caring, while others are shown as harmful. When touching is uncomfortable, Julie learns to say no and to tell a trusted adult. Proper anatomical terms are used.

Private Zone, Frances S. Dayee, Ill. by Marina Megale, Warner, 1984. Ages 3–8.

An informational book with sections for adults and children, written as a guide to protect children from sexual assault. Children are given an understanding of the privacy of their bodies and of the potential dangers to them, and they are encouraged to tell someone if they have been violated. This delicate subject is sensitively handled.

Take Care with Yourself: A Young Person's Guide to Understanding, Preventing, and Healing from the Hurts of Child Abuse, Laurie A. White and Steven L. Spencer, Ill. by Alice E. Cohen, Day Star Pr., 1983. Ages 4–8.

A nonfiction book in coloring book format that discusses feelings and emotions and the need to express them. Emotional, physical, and sexual abuse are defined, and what a child can do about them if they occur is described. The child's self-worth and right to be free from hurt are emphasized.

Problem-Related

Chilly Stomach, Jeannette Caines, Ill. by Pat Cummings, Harper, 1986. Ages 3–8.

Sandy does not like her Uncle Jim's hugs and kisses, but she is afraid to tell her parents. Sandy's revelation to a friend finally results in her decision to tell her parents. Circumstances prevent Sandy from telling her parents immediately, so the resolution is only implied. The picture book format used here may offer more reassurance to young children than do similar books.

Close to Home, Oralee Wachter, Ill. by Jane Aaron, Scholastic, 1986. Ages 5–10.

Four situations of potential child abduction are depicted in separate stories. One account involves a babysitter's friend, two are about strangers, and the last includes a noncustodial father. In each case, the children are confronted with making decisions regarding their personal safety.

Dial Zero for Help, Judith A. Jance, Ill. by Marina Megale, Franklin, 1985. Ages 5–8.

The anticipation of a fishing trip turns to anguish when Danny realizes that his father has abducted him. Danny is rescued by the police after he calls the operator for help. This fictional account of an abduction by a noncustodial parent is supplemented by an adult information section. *Highly recommended.*

Don't Hurt Me Mama, Muriel Stanek, Ill. by Helen Cogancherry, Albert Whitman, 1983. Ages 6–8.
A young girl describes her fear, isolation, and anxiety after her father's desertion. Her mother cannot find a job, begins drinking, and subsequently starts hitting her daughter. By telling the school nurse, the girl is able to get help for herself and for her mother. Recommended with reservations because the simple resolution seems implausible. Expressive illustrations.

Feeling Safe, Feeling Strong: How to Avoid Sexual Abuse and What to Do If It Happens to You, Susan N. Terkel and Janice E. Rench, Lerner, 1984. Ages 8–14.
Six fictional accounts by children about their experiences with sexual abuse, including pornography, incest, and a child's right not to kiss a relative. Following each story is information on the type of sexual abuse the story depicts and what a child can do to feel safe and strong. An excellent resource that can be adapted for younger children.

I Like You to Make Jokes with Me, I Don't Want You to Touch Me, Ellen Bass, Ill. by Marti Betz, Lollipop Power. 1981. Ages 3–7.
Sara enjoys grocery shopping with her mother. Joking with the grocer is fun, but his touch scares her. After practicing with her mother, Sarah learns to tell the man how she feels. He respects her wishes, and Sara is delighted with her newfound sense of inner strength.

It's Not Your Fault, Judith A. Jance, Ill. by Marina Megale, Franklin, 1985. Ages 5–8.
Last summer Terry was molested by Joe, her grandmother's husband. Fear of the loss of her mother's and grandmother's love keeps her from revealing the secret. But terrified by Joe's imminent visit, Terry finds the courage to tell and is reassured by her mother's love. Includes a parents' guide. Sensitive treatment of a delicate subject.

Liza's Story: Neglect and the Police, Deborah Anderson and Martha Finne, Ill. by Jeanette Swofford, Dillon, 1986. Ages 5–8.
Liza's mother has died, and her father lets her run wild. Her misbehavior escalates until she is taken to the police station. There her father's neglect is openly discussed. Through counseling, Liza's problem is gradually resolved. A separate section contains facts about child neglect. Recommended with reservations because the problem is so perfectly resolved.

Margaret's Story: Sexual Abuse and Going to Court, Deborah Anderson and Martha Finne, Ill. by Jeanette Swofford, Dillon, 1986. Ages 5–8.

A fictional account of a child who is molested by a trusted neighbor. Despite fear, Margaret tells her mother. With family support and the sensitive help of public officials, she is able to testify in court. Also included is a factual section for children and adults. Recommended with reservations because of its simplistic approach.

No More Secrets for Me, Oralee Wachter, Ill. by Jane Aaron, Little, 1983. Ages 4–8.

Four separate stories about varying types of degrees of sexual abuse. In each, the main character learns how to defend himself or herself by expressing his or her feelings and by confiding in someone he or she trusts. The intent of the book is to help children take care of themselves in the event of uncomfortable touching.

Safety Zone: A Book Teaching Child Abduction Prevention Skills, Linda D. Meyer, Ill. by Marina Megale, Franklin, 1984. Ages 4–10.

A nonfiction book about child abduction with sections for adults and children. The read-aloud part shows children in threatening circumstances, asks children to think about their reactions, and then describes a safe method of behavior. A realistic scenario of child abduction by a parent makes this book unique.

Strangers

The Dangers of Strangers, Carole Vogel and Kathryn Goldner, Ill. by Lynette Schmidt, Dillon, 1983. Ages 3–8.

A picture book that explains to children who is a stranger and that shows potentially harmful confrontations with strangers. Suggestions are given on how these situations should be handled. The book ends with a reassuring note to children about the safety and security of a loving family.

Never Say Yes to a Stranger: What Your Child Must Know to Stay Safe, Susan Newman, Photographs by George Tiboni, Perigee, 1985. Ages 7–12.

Ten different stories with photographs show early elementary-age children confronted by strangers and making mistakes that are dangerous to themselves. Each chapter is followed by safety tips on how the child should have reacted. The first two chapters can be used with preschool children. A parent guide is included.

Never Take Candy from Strangers, Rendy Beal, Ill. by Jeanne Seagle, RB Pubs., 1984. Ages 3–8.

An informative book with parental guidelines on how children can deal with strangers. Friends, acquaintances, and strangers are differentiated, but the focus is on people children do not know. Rules are given for avoiding strangers in public and at home. The best contribution of the book is its specific instructions on calling an operator for help.

Strangers, Dorothy Chlad, Ill. by Lydia Halverson, Childrens Pr., 1982. Ages 3–6.

Susie, a preschool child, tells about strangers. Safety rules for avoiding strangers and what to do if approached by one are given. This introductory book, intended to prevent child abduction, emphasizes that a stranger is anyone a child does not know.

Who Is a Stranger and What Should I Do?, Linda W. Girard, Ill. by Helen Cogancherry, Albert Whitman, 1985. Ages 5–10.

An informational book on how children should react to strangers. This book can be used to facilitate discussion between child and parent about rules regarding strangers. The text discusses characteristics of good and bad strangers, where one might encounter strangers, and rules on how to deal with them.

Related Titles

Problem-Related

Something Is Wrong at My House, Diane Davis.

Chapter 3

Death and Dying

Death of a Family Member or Friend
Death of a Pet
Funerals

The subject of death and dying is no longer taboo in our society, yet it is difficult to help children understand it. The event is devastating, whether it involves a pet, a famous figure, or a family member. Because of this, adults often try to protect children from the harsh realities of death or do not know how to discuss it with them. Books can help care-givers address this issue and avoid euphemisms in explaining the mean-ing of death. An honest discussion of the occurrence can prevent the child from imagining something more frightening than the truth. A child's concept of death is far different from that of an adult. Children from the ages of three to five tend to view death as temporary, not final. For children aged five to nine years, death is perceived as a person that is kept at a distance.

The fragmentation of families in today's society often prevents children from having a personal experience with death until they are much older. Exposure to this subject at an early age through books can help a child empathize with others who have experienced a death. Such exposure may also lessen the anxiety that accompanies grief when children finally do experience a death. Books can provide a bridge for adults and chil-dren to initiate conversation and to explore and express their feelings and fears concerning death.

The books described in this chapter were selected to help children un-derstand death. In the early '70s death was openly acknowledged as a part of the life cycle, and many children's books were written to aid them in coping with their grief and denial. Fewer books are being written to-day that help children incorporate death as a part of life. For this reason, and to ensure the quality of selections, we have included more books outside of the ten-year time frame here than in other chapters. It should also be noted that there is an obvious lack of books for young children on the death of a sibling and on suicide.

Death of a Family Member or Friend

About Dying: An Open Family Book for Parents and Children Together, Sara B. Stein, photographs by Dick Frank, Walker, 1974. Ages 5–8.

Although death is a part of life, the occurrence can be either hidden from or shared with a child. To encourage discussion, this author offers a text for children accompanied by one for adults. Through perceptive photographs and a simple style, the book describes the experiences three real children have with death.

Allison's Grandfather, Linda Peavy, Ill. by Ronald Himler, Scribner, 1981. Ages 6–10.

When Allison visits her grandparents in the summer, she and Erica become friends. Now Allison's grandfather is dying, and Erica remembers happy times spent with him. As Erica reminisces, she ponders the significance of death. Because of her fears, Erica does not discuss death with her parents until Allison's grandfather actually dies. *Highly recommended.*

Annie and the Old One, Miska Miles, Ill. by Peter Parnall, Little, 1971. Ages 5–8.

Annie's Navaho grandmother announces to her family that when the new rug is finished she will return to the earth (i.e., die). Because Annie cannot imagine life without "the Old One," she strives to prevent the weaving of the rug. However, Annie learns that she can neither hold back time nor the plan of nature.

Badger's Parting Gifts, Susan Varley, Lothrop, 1984. Ages 5–8.

Aged Badger accepts the inevitability of dying and tries to prepare his friends for his death. After his death, the grieving animals tell stories about the things Badger taught each one. In their sharing, they realize that their skills are gifts from Badger that they should treasure and pass on to others. Unique treatment of grief resolution.

Blackberries in the Dark, Mavis Jukes, Ill. by Thomas B. Allen, Knopf, 1985. Ages 7–10.

Austin's first visit to his grandmother since Grandpa's death begins awkwardly, since he resents Wayne, Grandmother's neighbor. Then Austin breaks Grandmother's antique doll's necklace. The grief and loneliness each feels are eased when they learn to fly-fish together and eat blackberries for supper. Before bedtime, Austin receives two treasured gifts, Grandmother's doll and Grandpa's fishing knife. *Highly recommended.*

Come Again in the Spring, Richard Kennedy, Ill. by Marcia Sewell, Harper, 1976. O.P. Ages 5–8.

Death, personified as a man, comes to visit Old Hark. Unprepared for the elderly man's resistance, Death wagers that Old Hark cannot answer questions about his early childhood and thereby live until spring. The birds Old Hark has fed daily help him make a successful bid for life until spring.

Dusty Was My Friend: Coming to Terms with Loss, Andrea Clardy, Ill. by Eleanor Alexander, Human Sci. Pr., 1984. Ages 6–10.

Eight-year-old Benjamin remembers his friend Dusty and Dusty's sudden death in a car accident. With a child's self-absorption, Benjamin describes his friendship with Dusty, his fears, and his grief. After a year, Benjamin finally accepts his loss. Simple yet poignant depiction of mourning.

The Empty Window, Eve Bunting, Ill. by Judy Clifford, Warne, 1980. O.P. Ages 8–12.

C.J. avoids visiting his best friend and classmate Joe, who is dying. Hearing about Joe's fascination for parrots, C.J. catches a wild one. He intends to just leave the bird, but suddenly C.J. finds himself in Joe's room. Discovering Joe's love of the parrot's freedom, C.J. frees it and resolves his fear of Joe's impending death.

Ⓡ ***Everett Anderson's Goodbye***, Lucille Clifton, Ill. by Ann Grifalconi, Holt, 1983. Ages 3–8.

Everett Anderson's father has died. His feelings demonstrate the five stages of grief—denial, anger, bargaining, depression, and, finally, loving acceptance. Each stage is simply and poignantly depicted on a single page. *Highly recommended.*

The Fall of Freddie the Leaf: A Story of Life for All Ages, Leo Buscaglia, Charles B. Slack, 1982. Ages 4 + .

An allegorical tale of the seasons of life. Through his wise friend Daniel, Freddie the Leaf learns of his reason for being and his uniqueness. He comes to understand that everyone will die, but death can be a beginning for new life. A gentle story accompanied by colorful photographs.

Ⓡ ***A Gift for Tia Rosa***, Karen T. Taha, Ill. by Dee de Rosa, Dillon, 1985. Ages 7–10.

Tia Rosa, Carmela's elderly neighbor, is dying. When Carmela finishes knitting a scarf for her father, she plans to make something for Tia Rosa. But Tia Rosa dies too soon. Carmela's mother teaches Carmela that she can pass on the love she had for Tia Rosa to those left behind.

Last Week My Brother Anthony Died, Martha W. Hickman, Ill. by Randie Julien, Abingdon, 1984. Ages 3–8.

Julie and her parents are trying to cope with the death of her four-week-old brother. This book sensitively portrays several concerns a preschool child has over the death of a sibling. A significant contribution in an area where little has been done at this age level.

Lifetimes: A Beautiful Way to Explain Death to Children, Bryan Mellonie, Ill. by Robert Ingpen, Bantham, 1983. O.P. Ages 4–8.

An introduction to the concept of death is presented in simple nonfiction text accompanied by vibrant illustrations of various life forms. The author emphasizes that for anything alive, there is a beginning and an ending, with "living in between." For all creatures, plants, animals, and people, death is a part of life.

My Grandmother Died, but I Won't Forget Her, Bernice Hogan, Ill. by Nancy Munger, Abingdon, 1983. Ages 4–8.

A gentle, straightforward story about a young boy whose grandmother has just died. He tells about the visitors who come to their home and about the funeral. The simple theme is that he misses his grandmother. Recalling their common bonds and seeking out reminders of her, the boy eases his loneliness.

My Grandpa Died Today, Joan Fassler, Ill. by Stuart Kranz, Human Sci. Pr., 1983. Ages 5–8.

David's grandfather tells him that he is not afraid to die because he knows that his grandson is not afraid to live. When his grandfather dies, David is engulfed with grief. Despite his loss, the memories of times shared with his grandfather help David discover his joy in living.

My Grandson Lew, Charlotte Zolotow, Ill. by William Pene DuBois, Harper, 1974. Ages 4–8.

Poignant reminiscences of a death not previously acknowledged between Lew and his mother. When Lew was two, his grandfather died. Now, four years later, Lew and his mother share memories in a quiet nighttime chat.

Nadia the Willful, Sue Alexander, Ill. by Lloyd Bloom, Pantheon, 1983. Ages 5–8.

Nadia's violent temper is calmed only by her brother Hamed. When he dies, their grieving father, the Sheik, forbids anyone to speak of Hamed. The silence increases Nadia's rage until she can't contain it. Her pain is eased by talking about Hamed, and Nadia teaches her father the importance of remembering.

Nana, Lyn L. Hoopes, Ill. by Arieh Zeldich, Harper, 1981. Ages 4–8.

An emptiness pervades Nana's house on the first morning after her death. A young girl keenly feels her loss, but when she goes outside and sees the signs of life in nature, the girl experiences the ever-present closeness of Nana. A sense of hope remains to ease her grief.

Nana Upstairs and Nana Downstairs, Tomie de Paola, Putnam, 1973. Ages 5–8.

A classic not to be missed. Sunday afternoons with his grandmother and great-grandmother are special to four-year-old Tommy. When Nana Upstairs, his great-grandmother, dies, Tommy's mother comforts him and gives him a way to say good-bye. Years later, Tommy says good-bye to his grandmother the same way.

Nonna, Jennifer Bartoli, Ill. by Joan Drescher, Harvey House, 1975. O.P. Ages 5–8.

A loving story is told by a young boy about his grandmother's death, funeral, and the family's grief. The tale takes place over a six-month time span and depicts the void left on special occasions when a family member dies and the importance of remembering the dead.

Sadako and the Thousand Paper Cranes, Eleanor Coerr, Ill. by Ronald Himler, Putnam, 1977. Ages 6–10.

Ten years after Hiroshima, Sadako dies from leukemia. As her once strong and active body feels the devastation of the disease, Sadako folds paper cranes for good luck and recovery. She dies surrounded by the love of her family and today is a heroine of Japanese children.

The Saddest Time, Norma Simon, Ill. by Jacqueline Rogers, Albert Whitman, 1986. Ages 5–8.

Three separate vignettes about death. In the first, a boy describes the death of his young uncle; in the second, classmates reminisce about a friend; and in the final story, a young girl reflects on the death of her grandmother. Each story offers a means of coping and coming to terms with grief.

Talking about Death: A Dialogue between Parent and Child, Earl A. Grollman, Beacon, 1976. Ages 5–9.

The picture book section of this book can be used to help answer children's questions about death, dying, and the emotions of bereavement. This section is expanded upon in an extensive parents' guide to help parents and their children cope with the grief process.

A Taste of Blackberries, Doris B. Smith, Ill. by Charles Robinson, Crowell, 1973. Ages 6–10.

A boy tells of his wonderful, lively best friend Jamie and the pain of losing this special person to tragedy. An impulsive, seemingly harmless gesture ends in guilt, grief, and a slow recovery for the young narrator. *Highly recommended.*

Time for Uncle Joe, Nancy Jewell, Ill. by Joan Sandin, Harper, 1981. Ages 4–8.

The changing seasons evoke fond memories of Uncle Joe for a young girl. Although he has died, Uncle Joe's spirit lives on through the wonders of nature and through the belongings he left with his family. Finally, the young girl is able to put away her uncle's things and say good-bye.

® *The Two of Them*, Aliki, Greenwillow, 1979. Ages 4–8.
A tribute to the love between a grandfather and his granddaughter. Grandfather sings lullabies, tells tales, and teaches his granddaughter to garden. After Grandfather becomes ill, the child tells stories and sings songs to him. When he dies, the girl hurts "inside and out," but she knows she will not forget him. *Highly recommended.*

We Remember Philip, Norma Simon, Ill. by Ruth Sanderson, Albert Whitman, 1979. Ages 6–9.
Sam and his friends regard Mr. Hall as a very special teacher. When Mr. Hall's son Philip dies in an accident, Sam and the other students gently help him move through his mourning. Before the school year is over, they find a way to commemorate Philip.

When Grandfather Journeys into Winter, Craig K. Strete, Ill. by Hal Frenck, Greenwillow, 1979. O.P. Ages 7–10.
Tayhua has taught his grandson, Little Thunder, the Indian ways. Now, after riding and winning a wild stallion for the boy, Tayhua lies on his deathbed. Little Thunder rails against parting, but Tayhua helps him accept the inevitable. Little Thunder comes to understand that Tayhua will always be with him, even after death.

When Grandpa Came to Stay, Judith Caseley, Greenwillow, 1986. Ages 5–7.
It is Grandpa Levy's first visit since Grandma died. Benny loves the visit until Grandpa cries. Angry at first over Grandpa's tears, Benny learns that adults can be sad and cry. Grandpa does not hide his mourning but takes Benny to the cemetery to say hello to Grandma.

When People Die, Joanne E. Bernstein and Stephen V. Gallo, photographs by Rosemarie Hausherr, Dutton, 1977. O.P. Ages 5–8.
The death of Mrs. Michaelson, an 82-year-old, provides a starting point for this nonfiction book describing death, dying, religious beliefs, funerals, and the grieving process. Death is presented factually as a part of the cycle of life, as is acknowledging the grief it brings.

Where's Jess?, Joy and Marv Johnson, Ill. by Shari Barum, Centering Corp., 1982. Ages 3–6.
Following the death of her baby brother, the narrator questions her parents about the meaning of "dead." They explain Jess' death and reassure the girl that she is not responsible for his death. The family misses Jess, but they openly share their feelings, remembering him. The book deals well with a preschooler's concerns about a sibling's death.

Death of a Pet

The Accident, Carol Carrick, Ill. by Donald Carrick, Houghton, 1976. Ages 4–8.

On his way to meet his parents, Christopher sees his dog, Bodger, killed by a truck. When Christopher's parents arrive, they are not angry with the driver, so Christopher's grief is compounded by his rage at his parents. Finding a special way to honor Bodger and some time for sadness help Christopher resolve the dilemma. A sequel, *The Foundling*, by the same author is included later in this chapter.

The Black Dog Who Went into the Woods, Edith T. Hurd, Ill. by Emily A. McCully, Harper, 1980. Ages 5–8.

As the story begins, Benjamin, the youngest child, announces that Black Dog has gone into the woods to die. The unbelieving family goes futilely to search for him. Gradually, the family comes to accept Black Dog's death. One quiet night, as the family members sleep, Black Dog comes to each in their dreams to say good-bye.

Do You Love Me?, Dick Gackenbach, Houghton, 1975. Ages 5–8.

Walter is lonely, and his pets, some bugs and turtles, do not offer him companionship. Fascinated by a hummingbird, he tries to catch it and accidentally kills it. After a discussion with his sister about respecting animals, a contrite Walter sets his pets free. His sister then brings him a puppy.

The Foundling, Carol Carrick, Ill. by Donald Carrick, Houghton, 1977. Ages 4–8.

Young Christopher finds life lonely without his pet dog, Bodger. No dog can replace him in Christopher's heart, not even the lively puppy at the animal shelter. Just when Christopher reiterates that he doesn't want another dog, he rescues a homeless puppy, who captures the boy's love. A sequel to *The Accident* by the same author.

I'll Always Love You, Hans Wilhelm, Crown, 1985. Ages 3–8.

A young boy describes his relationship with Elfie, the best dog in the world. But as the boy grows tall, Elfie gets old and one morning is found dead. The narrator is comforted by remembering that every evening he told her, "I'll always love you." A poignant story of grief and love.

Jim's Dog Muffins, Miriam Cohen, Ill. by Lillian Hoban, Greenwillow, 1984. Ages 5–8.

The first-graders are sorry that their classmate Jim's dog, Muffins, has died. Their sympathy wavers, however, when Jim is silent, even hostile to their attempts to console him. Their teacher explains that Jim needs time to be sad. Jim finally finds solace as he and his friend Paul laugh, cry, and talk about Muffins. *Highly recommended*.

Mustard, Charlotte Graeber, Ill. by Donna Diamond, Macmillian, 1982. Ages 6–10.

Mustard is the family's beloved cat. She is 14, but Alex cannot bear to hear that she is old. A visit to the vet reveals heart problems, and everyone must deal with Mustard's illness. For any pet owner who must face the grief of putting an animal to sleep.

Petey, Tobi Tobias, Ill. by Symeon Shimin, Putnam, 1978. O.P. Ages 5–8.

Petey, Emily's pet gerbil, becomes sick. Despite a night-long vigil, Emily finds Petey dead in the morning. The end of such a special relationship is not easy to bear, despite the family's loving support. In time, Emily accepts an offer of new gerbils and has a different but good experience.

Stories from a Snowy Meadow, Carla Stevens, Ill. by Eve Rice, Houghton, 1976. O.P. Ages 5–8.

Four stories about Mole, Shrew, and Mouse, and their many kindnesses to aging Vole. Vole reciprocates by sharing her experiences and wisdom with them. In the final chapter, the three friends grieve at the death of Vole, but Mouse helps them understand the legacy she has left behind.

The Tenth Good Thing about Barney, Judith Viorst, Ill. by Erik Blegvad, Atheneum, 1971. Ages 4–8.

Although very sad when his cat Barney dies, a young boy thinks of nine good things to say about him at the funeral. After much thought, the grieving boy discovers a tenth good thing about Barney, perhaps the most lasting of all.

Whiskers Once and Always, Doris Orgel. Ill. by Carol Newsom, Viking/ Penguin, 1986. Ages 7–10.

Becky's cat, Whiskers, dies. She cannot express grief until she is with her friends, but then Jason, a classmate, makes a callous remark. His words cause her additional emotional turmoil, and in a reflexive action, Becky punches Jason. A look at the impact wrought by a beloved pet's death.

Funerals

The Happy Funeral, Eve Bunting, Ill. by Vo-Dinh Mai, Harper, 1982. Ages 5–9.

Laura's Chinese-American family is preparing for her grandfather's funeral. When her mother tells her it will be a happy funeral, this seems a contradiction. However, Laura comes to realize that the happiness is for her grandfather, who lived a good life, not for his family.

Tell Me, Papa, Joy and Marv Johnson, Ill. by Shari Borum, Centering Corp., 1978. Ages 6–8.

A grandfather speaks to children of funerals and of saying good-bye to a loved one who has died. Death is shown as irrevocable, and the preparation of the body for the funeral is described. The feelings of those left behind are also discussed. A small press publication for children about funerals.

Related Titles

Death of a Family Member or Friend

Harry's Mom, Barbara Porte.

Oliver Hyde's Dishcloth Concert, Richard Kennedy.

Chapter 4

Difficult Situations

Going to School
Loss of an Object or Pet
Moving
Temporary Separation

Change is difficult for everyone, but especially for young children. They derive security from structure and familiar routines. Every day, parents are faced with the challenge of helping children to prepare for a new situation or to resolve the anxiety associated with change. Although not as catastrophic as death and divorce, changes such as moving can pose difficult challenges for young children. Often the events are positive, but the transition still can be stressful.

Moving and going to school for the first time are seen by adults as common occurrences, but they may be perceived by a child as threatening. Minor changes, such as having a babysitter or losing a favorite toy, can also be overwhelming. Alterations in a child's daily activities can cause fears and insecurities to surface. At times, these feelings may be reflected in the child's behavior. For instance, a child who rebels against a babysitter may actually be concerned that his or her parents will not return.

Faced with these difficult situations, children can gain reassurance and learn coping skills from books. Stories can help a child identify with a character who is experiencing his or her unique problem and demonstrate options for resolution. A child's fears thus may be decreased by learning that his or her anxieties are shared by other children.

By anticipating or perceiving a child's stress in a specific situation, an adult can provide a book to initiate conversation. This involvement may be especially important because the child may not realize that he or she is experiencing a specific anxiety, or the child may be unable to verbally express his or her distress. Books can help a child who is experiencing these difficult situations and can also reinforce the child/adult interaction. Finally, the resolution of feelings concerning a difficult transition can help prepare the child for a lifetime of changes. Books included in this chapter were selected because they deal with the most common transitions and losses encountered by children.

Going to School

Adam Smith Goes to School, Bernard Wolf, Lippincott, 1978. Ages 4–7.

Six-year-old Adam Smith is starting first grade. There are serious and fun things to learn and do, and rules to follow. Black-and-white photographs chronicle the events in Adam's first days at school. The simple text reveals the joys and challenges he must face.

The Bad Dreams of a Good Girl, Susan Shreve, Ill. by Diane de Groat, 1982. Ages 7–10.

What would you do if shortly after you started attending a new school someone formed the I Hate Lotty Club? Lotty is the youngest and only girl in the McDaniel family, and she has always been a good girl. But sometimes Lotty has bad daydreams, as revealed in the four anecdotes that comprise each chapter.

Betsy's First Day at Nursery School, Gunilla Wolde, Random, 1976. Ages 3–6.

Attending nursery school doesn't seem like a good idea to Betsy, but she goes to visit. Because of her fears, Betsy thinks that the children are staring at her and has other negative reactions. A little girl sticks her tongue out at Betsy, and Betsy does the same, but soon they are laughing. Betsy gradually learns to adapt to her new role as student.

First Day of School, Helen Oxenbury, Dial, 1983. Ages 2^1/2–4.

A little girl clings to her mother as they arrive at nursery school. Hesitant at first, she soon becomes involved with the other children, teachers, and activities. Delightful, humorous illustrations capture the foibles of this age group.

Going to Day Care, Fred Rogers, photographs by Jim Judkins, Putnam, 1985. Ages 3–6.

A nonfiction book with brightly colored photographs depicting the experiences children will encounter in day care. Children are reassured that although families love each other, they cannot always be together. Although playing and sharing, and eating and napping away from home can be difficult, this book can help ease the transition.

I Don't Want to Go to School, Elizabeth Bram, Greenwillow, 1977. Ages 4–6.

On the first day of kindergarten, Jennifer has many reasons not to go: a sick doll, no perfect dress, and missing shoes. An understanding mother and the laughter of children going to school lure Jennifer to a happy new experience. Simple text and pictures gently portray a common childhood experience.

The I Don't Want to Go to School Book, Alan Gross, Ill. by Mike Venezia, Childrens Pr., 1982. Ages 5–8.

The common anxieties children face at school are recounted. The young narrator seems to have many reasons to stay home and miss school. After much thought, however, he decides that the benefits of attending school are greater than a day spent at home and rushes out the door.

I Started School Today, Karen Frandsen, Childrens Pr., 1984. Ages 4–7.

A small boy starts school but is worried that a stranger might steal his toys and that the burden of learning to read will be too much for him. Neither trouble occurs on the first day, and he decides that he likes his teacher and makes a friend. A light, humorous look at children's anxieties about attending school.

My First Days of School, Jane Hamilton-Merritt, Simon & Schuster, 1982. Ages 4–6.

Five-year-old Kate is preparing to start school. With her stuffed animal, Bear, as a constant companion, Kate tells about the adjustment of being a first-time student. After a few days, Kate is secure enough to leave Bear at home. An informational book with black-and-white photographs.

My Nursery School, Harlow Rockwell, Greenwillow, 1976. Ages 2–4.

A young child describes her nursery school, ranging from classmates to activities. Few words and simple illustrations allow for very young children to identify with the experiences portrayed in this informational picture book.

The New Girl at School, Judy Delton, Ill. by Lillian Hoban, Dutton, 1979. Ages 5–8.

The transition to a new school is difficult for the young narrator, who here describes her feelings of being an outsider in her new class. By the end of the first week, however, she finds acceptance and acknowledgement by her classmates.

Nursery School, Harold Roth, Grosset, 1986. Ages 2–4.

A board book focusing on the activities encountered at nursery school: exercising, coloring, cooking, and listening to stories. Brightly colored photographs show a multiracial class having fun. Only positive experiences are included.

Starting School, Muriel Stanek, Ill. by Betty and Tony DeLuna, Albert Whitman, 1981. Ages 4–6.

A young boy prepares to enter school, including learning new skills and visiting the doctor and dentist. He then tells what the first day of school is like and describes his teachers and classmates, the things he learns, and the rules he has to follow. He leaves school that day with a new sense of independence.

When You Go to Kindergarten, James Howe, photographs by Betsy Imershein, Knopf, 1986. Ages 5–6.

This nonfiction book accompanied by black-and-white photographs is a positive exposure to this childhood milestone. Besides explaining the many details of kindergarten life, the book reassuringly describes a child's possible emotional reactions to school. The challenges of riding a school bus, using suitable behavior, and following a fire drill are included.

Willy Bear, Mildred Kantrovitz, Ill. by Nancy W. Parker, Parents Mag. Pr., 1976. O.P. Ages 4–7.

It's a busy night as a little boy transfers his anxieties about starting school to his stuffed animal, Willy Bear. Tending to his bear's needs helps this child cope with the demands of growing up. Morning's realities are eased by his pretending that his going to the first day of school is done for Willy Bear's sake.

Loss of an Object or Pet

The Comeback Dog, Jane R. Thomas, Ill. by Troy Howell, Houghton, 1981. Ages 7–12.

Daniel still grieves for his dog Captin when he finds Lady, a nearly dead English setter. Despite all of his tender care, she does not love him as Captin did. Daniel finally sets her free and again feels terrible loneliness. But Lady does return, needing his care and love.

David and Dog, Shirley Hughes, Prentice-Hall, 1981. Ages 4–7.

David and his toy, Dog, are inseparable. Bella, David's sister, sleeps with seven teddy bears, but David needs only Dog. When Dog becomes lost, David becomes distraught. The next day, Dog is mistakenly sold to a girl at a school fair. However, due to Bella's generosity, David and Dog are reunited. *Highly recommended*.

I Don't Care, Marjorie W. Sharmat, Ill. by Lillian Hoban, Macmillan, 1977. Ages 3–5.

This book emphasizes that grief for any lost object cannot be denied. Jonathan has lost his wonderful balloon, yet he proclaims that he doesn't care. He learns that even such a seemingly small loss must be acknowledged before it can be resolved.

Lost in the Storm, Carol Carrick, Ill. by Donald Carrick, Clarion, 1974. Ages 5–8.

Christopher and his dog, Bodger, go to visit Christopher's friend Gray at his island home. As a storm begins, the boys go into the house, but

Bodger is lost. Christopher spends a long, anxious night. An early morning search ends in a joyful reunion. A companion to *The Accident* and *The Foundling* by the same author.

The Summer Cat, Howard Knotts, Harper, 1981. Ages 5–8.

The calico cat, a mysterious evening visitor, first appears to Ben perched in the apple tree. Over the summer, Ben grows to love her very much and names her Apple Blossom. But at summer's end, he relinquishes her to her owner, the summer lady. Ben and Apple Blossom dream of next summer.

When Lucy Went Away, G. Max Ross, Ill. by Ingrid Fetz, Dutton, 1976. Ages 4–8.

Lucy the cat goes along with her family to their summer place. She follows the children everywhere. When it is time to return home, Lucy is gone. Searching and worrying do not bring her back. Although the family leaves without her, they hope she will be safe and happy.

The Witch Who Lost Her Shadow, Mary Calhoun, Ill. by Trinka H. Noble, Harper, 1979. Ages 4–8.

Falinda, a good witch, is constantly followed by her independent, non-affectionate cat, Shadow. One day he disappears, and Falinda futilely searches for him. The villagers offer her many cats, but none is acceptable. A kitten, whose personality is completely opposite to Shadow's, pursues Falinda until he fills the void in her heart.

Moving

® *Angel Child, Dragon Child*, Michele M. Surat, Ill. by Vo-Dinh Mai, Raintree, 1983. Ages 5–9.

Ut, a Vietnamese child, is teased at school for being different. Not only must she adjust to a new country, but she is also lonely for her mother, who has been left behind. When her greatest enemy, Raymond, becomes her special friend, they devise a way to bring Ut's mother to America. Beautiful illustrations.

® *The Big Hello*, Janet Schulman, Ill. by Lillian Hoban, Greenwillow, 1976; Dell, 1980. Ages 6–8. Greenwillow Read-alone.

A young girl making a cross-country move projects her fears onto her rag doll, Sara. Comforting Sara mitigates the trip and lack of friends, but then Sara is lost. The girl's new dog, Snoopy, helps her find Sara and make a friend as well.

City, Sing for Me: A Country Child Moves to the City, Jane Jacobson, Ill. by Amy Rowen, Human Sci. Pr., 1978. Ages 6–10.

When Jenny moves to the city, the country's singing birds and clear blue sky are replaced by booming noises and crowding. Everything seems cold and foreign until Jenny meets Rosa, who shows her the wonderful smells and sights found at bakeries, delicatessens, and parks. Jenny's view of the city changes to a more promising one.

® *Gila Monsters Meet You at the Airport*, Marjorie W. Sharmat, Ill. by Byron Barton, Penguin, 1980. Ages 4–8.

A small boy discusses why he does not want to move from his home in New York to the West. The reasons he gives are fantasies of exaggerated stereotypes. Before he completes the move, the boy discovers the absurdity of his beliefs.

I'm Moving, Martha W. Hickman, Abingdon, 1974. O.P. Ages 3–6.

William's family is in the process of moving to a new home. Before the move, his parents discuss what can be moved and what is to be left behind. The move is a success. New things—friends, trees, sidewalks—replace the losses, and William still has his mommy, daddy, baby brother, and turtle. A companion to *My Friend William Moved Away* by the same author.

I'm Not Moving!, Penelope Jones, Ill. by Amy Aitken, Bradbury Pr., 1980. O.P. Ages 5–7.

Emmy doesn't want to go when her family moves. She searches for someplace to stay. At one neighbor's, she doesn't like the food; at another's, the cat bothers her. She decides to live in her digging hole, but her parents' promise of a new hole lures Emmy into accepting the move.

Jenny's Cat, Miska Miles, Ill. by Wendy Watson, Dutton, 1979. O.P. Ages 6–10.

Nothing is right after Jenny's family moves—there are no friends, Papa travels, and Mama needs reassurance. Jenny is forlorn until a stray cat, Patches, comes into her life. Now realizing that Patches is pregnant, Mama and Papa want to take the cat to a farm. Jenny's love for Patches triumphs.

The Monster in the Third Dresser Drawer, Janice Smith, Ill. by Dick Gackenbach, Harper, 1981. Ages 5–8.

Six independent stories portray the traumas in the life of young Adam Joshua. Adam finds that there is nothing trivial about a move, making room for a new sister, discovering a monster in the dresser, or enduring elderly relatives. Many children will identify with this literal-minded character.

Moving Day, Tobi Tobias, Ill. by William Pene DuBois, Knopf, 1976. Ages 3–5.

A fast-paced story of a young girl and her teddy bear experiencing the family's move. The hustle and bustle of packing, saying good-bye, and the actual move are succinctly expressed. However, the story reflects little of the trauma or uncertainties involved in moving.

Moving Molly, Shirley Hughes, Prentice-Hall, 1979. Ages 5–8.

When Molly's family moves to the country, her brother and sister start school, but she is too young to do so. Molly therefore is left to entertain herself and is lonely. When twins move in next door, Molly finds herself busy because she has found friends. Contains detailed illustrations for the very young.

My Best Friend Moved Away, Joy Zelon, Raintree, 1980. Ages 5–8.

When Nick's family decides to move, his best friend Brian becomes so upset that he tries to destroy the "For Sale" sign in front of the house. Brian is lonely without Nick; but after visiting him, Brian finds that Nick has changed. With his father's help, Brian learns how people can grow apart.

My Friend William Moved Away, Martha W. Hickman, Ill. by Bill Myers, Abingdon, 1979. Ages 4–8.

Best friends William and Jimmy have many things in common. When William moves away, he leaves Jimmy with all the familiar things except his best friend. A day of missing his friend ends happily, however, when Jimmy discovers Mary Ellen, who has been there all along. A sequel to *I'm Moving* by the same author.

New Neighbors for Nora, Johanna Hurwitz, Ill. by Susan Jeschke, Morrow, 1979. Ages 5–8.

Nora looks forward to playing with two new children in her apartment building, but nothing turns out as she expects. Her neighbor Russell's baby sister is too little to play, and Nora is even more disgruntled to learn that her other new neighbor is the unbearable Eugene. Gradually, Nora and Eugene become friends.

Nice New Neighbors, Franz Brandenberg, Ill. by Aliki, Scholastic, 1980. Ages 4–8.

The six Fieldmouse children are rebuffed when they try to make friends in their new neighborhood. Their mother keeps telling them that some day the other children will know better. That day comes sooner than expected when the other children beg to be involved in the Fieldmouses' play.

The Potters' Kitchen, Rachel Isadora, Greenwillow, 1977. O.P. Ages 5–8.

The Potters are happy in their home in the country, but Mr. Potter gets a new job in the city. Saddened, they move into their new apartment where Samantha and Jonathan each make friends in their own way. As in the country, the kitchen in their city apartment is still the hub of their existence.

The Trip, Ezra J. Keats, Greenwillow, 1978. Ages 4–8.

A move to a new neighborhood leaves Louie with no friends. Through his imagination, he returns to his old friends and their camaraderie on Halloween. He is recalled to the present when his mother comes to help him with his costume, and he goes off to join the other "Trick or Treaters."

We Are Best Friends, Aliki, Greenwillow, 1982. Ages 4–8.

How can a best friend move away?, wonders Robert. Without Peter, there is no one with whom Robert can fight, as well as play. Robert is angry and will not make friends with a new boy until he receives a letter from Peter. Then he is able to understand the many degrees of friendship.

Temporary Separation

Alfie Gets in First, Shirley Hughes, Lothrop, 1981. Ages 4–7.

Arriving home from shopping, mother sets the groceries in the hall and goes outside for Annie Rose. Alfie, already in the house, slams the door and locks mother outside. When Alfie cannot open the door, the whole neighborhood gets involved in solving the problem, but Alfie surprises them all.

All Alone after School, Muriel Stanek, Ill. by Ruth Rosner, Albert Whitman, 1985. Ages 6–9.

When Josh's mother must go to work, she helps him get ready to be alone after school. They make lists of phone numbers and safety rules. Despite the preparations, Josh is lonely and nervous on his first day home alone. As time passes, he enjoys the benefits and responsibilities of being alone.

Bus Ride, Nancy Jewell, Ill. by Ronald Himler, Harper, 1978. O.P. Ages 4–8.

The new experience of a long bus ride without her parents is highlighted for Janie by kindly Mrs. Rivers, her traveling companion. Details of bus travel are interspersed with new friendships and exciting scenery. Janie's initial anxieties are replaced with the ambivalence of leaving Mrs. Rivers and greeting Grandpa.

Don't Forget to Come Back, Robie H. Harris, Ill. by Tony DeLuna, Knopf, 1978. O.P. Ages 3–7.

Annie first learns that her parents are going out when she hears her mother call Bob, the babysitter. Annie is furious, but pleading, temper tantrums, and hiding do not alter the situation. Annie is finally resigned to her parents going, kisses them good night, and reminds them to come back home.

An Evening at Alfie's, Shirley Hughes, Lothrop, 1984. Ages 4–8.
After Maureen, the babysitter, reads about Noah and his ark, Alfie goes to bed. Later, the dripping sound he hears is not from remembering the story, but from a burst water pipe, which soon has Alfie and Maureen scurrying. Peace is restored when Maureen's parents come to the rescue.

George the Babysitter, Shirley Hughes, Prentice-Hall, 1975. Ages 4–8.
Mother goes to work, and George comes to babysit for Mike, Jenny, and Baby Sue. Together they share chores and fun activities, some successful and others with less optimal results. A busy day ends with happiness and relief for George.

Harry's Visit, Barbara A. Porte, Ill. by Yossi Abolafia, Greenwillow, 1983. Ages 6–8. Greenwillow Read-alone.
Harry's visit to his father's friends does not begin well. He doesn't like the food and has nothing in common with the child closest to him in age. The day improves when Harry is invited to play basketball. Children facing similar new situations can appreciate how Harry's sense of humor saves his day.

Home Alone, Eleanor Schick, Dial, 1980. Ages 6–8. Dial Easy-to-read.
Careful planning by a mother helps her son deal with his first experience of going home to an empty house after school. His potential fears and loneliness are alleviated by his parents' rules for safety and by his pet cat and toys. Comforting reading for the latchkey child and parent.

Martin by Himself, Gloria Skurzynski, Ill. by Lynn Munsinger, Houghton, 1979. O.P. Ages 6–8.
It is mother's first day at work and Martin's first day to arrive home with no one there. In one short hour, Martin almost demolishes the house with Gus, the neighbor's dog. Despite his mother's anguished amazement, she understands the reason for the disarray. Together, Martin and his mother work out a solution.

My Mom Travels a Lot, Caroline F. Bauer, Ill. by Nancy W. Parker, Warne, 1981. Ages 4–8.
A picture book about a child who is cared for by her father while her mother travels. The girl recounts the good and bad things about her mother's absence. The book ends with a reassuring note for any child in

the same predicament: "The best thing about it is she always comes back."

The Sweeneys from 9-D, Ethel and Leonard Kessler, Macmillan, 1985. Ages 6–8. Ready-to-read.

Too many things are new in the lives of the three Sweeney children. While mother goes off to work, the children face the challenge of switching schools, making friends, and assuming responsibilities. An anxious and sometimes dismal day ends happily for the latchkey children.

Visting Pamela, Norma Klein, Ill. by Kay Chorao, Dial, 1979. Ages 4–8.

Five-year-old Carrie doesn't like visiting her friends' homes. She prefers Mommy and home, where everything is safe and under control. A visit to her friend Pamela's starts unpleasantly and is vividly described by Carrie. When Mommy arrives to rescue Carrie, things have changed for the better.

Waiting, Nicki Weiss, Greenwillow, 1981. Ages 3–6.

Mother promises AnnaLee that she'll be back before she is missed. AnnaLee's wait by the gate is endless, interrupted by many things that cause AnnaLee to think Mama has returned. Finally, the promise comes true.

You Go Away, Dorothy Corey, Ill. by Lois Axeman, Albert Whitman, 1976. Ages 2–4.

Through a variety of separation experiences ranging from the momentary to the prolonged, preschool children are reassured that their parents will return. Few words and colorful illustrations of children of different races demonstrate the separations that create anxiety at different ages.

Your First Airplane Trip, Pat and Joel Ross, Ill. by Lynn Wheeling, Lothrop, 1981. Ages 4–8.

The book contains exacting details of air travel, ranging from the initial check-in at the airport to arrival at the destination. A sure way to reassure and introduce the novice to commercial flying. An informative book.

Related Titles

Moving
Sunny-Side Up, Patricia R. Giff.

Temporary Separation
Alfie Gives a Hand, Shirley Hughes.

Chapter 5

Emotions and Feelings

Anger
Bad Days
Expressing Feelings
General
    Embarrassment
    Generosity
    Hatred
    Loneliness
    Sadness
    Security
    Selfishness
    Shyness
Greed
Jealousy
Joy
Love
Serenity

From earliest childhood, emotions play an integral part of every person's life. They are intricate and subjective responses affecting not only our personal functioning, but also how we interact with others. Every reaction to the outside world and many of our decisions about the world around us are colored by our emotions. The ability to label these emotions helps us deal with them on a personal level and is essential for true communication. This ability to identify and articulate feelings evolves over time and through experience.

Young children quickly realize the importance of emotions, but they cannot adequately verbalize them. Gradually, as they observe and imitate people around them, children learn to express their feelings. Ideally, they should discuss their feelings with those whom they model themselves after. When this interaction occurs, it is the adult's responsibility to give as much attention to children's emotional development as they give to children's motor and intellectual growth.

It is important that a child's emotional "learning" is not separated from

38

other forms of learning. For instance, a baby's frustration with immobility is essential for learning to walk. As parents applaud the child's first steps, they must also acknowledge the emotional impact their responses has on the child. At all stages in a child's life, it is essential for adults to understand the emotional turmoil that accompanies each challenge.

Just as it is essential not to criticize children who are mastering a new skill, adults should avoid dictating how children should feel. Children do not need judgment; rather, they need help in dealing with their emotional experiences. It is the role of caregivers to be aware of children as individuals, to support and respect their emotional development.

As children are confronted with feelings and emotions, whether positive or negative, adults need to be cognizant of certain verbal and nonverbal clues. Often, for example, children may throw tantrums, demonstrate rage, or repress or conceal their feelings. Parents should recognize that the need to control an unacceptable demonstration of emotion does not negate the existence of those feelings. It is crucial to recognize feelings and not deny them. Expressing emotions in a constructive manner reduces the negative consequences they can have on a child's long-term health. An empathetic caregiver can help a child express feelings through words and diffuse potential stress and outbursts. Caregivers should use every method available to help children understand and express their feelings.

Reading is a common approach to helping children identify, experience, and express emotions. There may be times when books are shared with children because they relate to the behaviors being exhibited. At other times, books can be a means to helping children learn how to express their emotions. Through reading and discussion, children can be helped to understand that emotions have a cause-and-effect relationship, and they have a chance to examine the consequences of displaying certain emotions. When emotions become problematic, books can be a source of comfort for children. Identification with a book's character can help children to see their situation more clearly and foster a resolution of their emotional conflict.

Books can assist caregivers in helping children understand their emotional selves and in helping children appreciate the emotional responses and needs of others. Communication on this subject, started at an early age, can aid children in avoiding the discomfort that many adults have in expressing their feelings. Stories can facilitate discussion between children and adults, starting in the preschool years.

There is a wealth of children's books dealing with emotions and feelings. Unfortunately, many of these are pedantic "self-help" books. We have chosen only the books that we feel will enhance the emotional development of children. By comparing various books, adults can discover those of quality that may be the most appropriate for the child in their care.

Anger

Gilly Gilhooley: A Tale of Ireland, Arnold Dobrin, Crown, 1976. O.P. Ages 6–9.

When Gilly Gilhooley goes out into the world, his parents enjoin him not to lose his temper and to remember the laughter within himself. Nevertheless, Gilly loses two jobs because of his anger. On the third job, he finally learns to control his temper and gets what he wants by using his humor.

Rollo and Juliet, Marjorie W. Sharmat, Ill. by Marylin Hafner, Doubleday, 1981. O.P. Ages 5–8.

Rollo Cat and Juliet Cat vow to be friends forever. When Rollo forgets their game of tag, an incensed Juliet initiates a fight, and Rollo retaliates. Both cats thrive on their anger, but after a few weeks and some misguided attempts at reconciliation, they renew their undying friendship.

Sara and the Door, Virginia A. Jensen, Ill. by Ann Strugnell, Addison-Wesley, 1977. O.P. Ages 3–6.

Tears and temper don't help Sara when she closes the door and catches her coat in it. She is too small to reach the knob, and no one comes when she calls for help. Sara finally extricates herself by learning to unbutton her coat. Monochromatic illustrations capture Sara's emotions, ranging from anger to satisfaction.

Bad Days

Awful Thursday, Ron Roy, Ill. by Lillian Hoban, Pantheon, 1979. Ages 6–8. An I am reading book.

Jack is excited when his teacher lends him a tape recorder, but his good fortune turns into disaster when he fears that a bus has run over it. Left with a smashed bag, he anguishes over what to tell his teacher. Much to his relief, it is Jack who receives an apology.

Friday the 13th, Steven Kroll, Ill. by Dick Gackenbach, Holiday, 1981. Ages 5–8.

Hilda never misses a chance to point out her brother Harold's misfortunes. Harold therefore expects Friday the 13th to be a disaster. Despite his usual bad luck, Harold responds to cheering from his team's fans and wins the game. When Hilda makes a mess, his day is complete.

Today Was a Terrible Day, Patricia R. Giff, Ill. by Susanna Natti, Viking, 1980. Ages 5–8.

Second-grader Ronald Morgan eats a classmate's lunch, misses a catch in a baseball game, and cannot read a simple sentence. After his disaster-prone day, Ronald feels very down until he successfully reads a note from his concerned teacher. Illustrations capture Ronald's emotions, ranging from despair to jubilance. *Highly recommended.*

Up Day, Down Day, Jacquie Hann, Four Winds Pr., 1978. Ages 4–7.

The narrator and his friend Jeremy go fishing. He catches a cold; Jeremy catches three fish. Jeremy is lucky until Monday, when he goes to school and takes a test while his friend stays home and plays. In a humorous ending, the friends exchange a cold for a fish.

Wet Monday, Dorothy Edwards, Ill. by Jenny Williams, Morrow, 1976. O.P. Ages 4–7.

One rainy Monday, mom, dad, brother, sister, and dog, Toby, are all disgruntled. There are quarrels before they leave the house, and Toby is not taken out. The day becomes progressively worse for each. The family returns to the chaos Toby has wrought, and as they share laughter, the gloomy day brightens.

Expressing Feelings

Ⓡ *Feelings*, Aliki, Greenwillow, 1984. Ages 4–8.

Numerous vignettes demonstrate the emotions of anger, love, jealousy, sadness, and many others. The author succinctly portrays such experiences as a young boy's joy because of a party invitation and a girl's jealousy of a curly-haired child. The cartoon-like illustrations tenderly depict many of humanity's foibles. *Highly recommended.*

I Hate Kisses, Robie H. Harris, Ill. by Diane Paterson, Knopf, 1981. Ages 4–7.

Peter gives his favorite stuffed toy, Nellie, to his father and informs his parents that he hates kisses. He has determined that he is too old for both things. Peter replaces Nellie's companionship with a shiny new robot and rejects his parents' affection. An incident at bedtime causes Peter to reconsider his thinking.

Jafta, Hugh Lewin, Ill. by Lisa Kopper, Carolrhoda, 1983. Ages 3–7.

Jafta, a little African boy, explains his feelings of happiness, tiredness, and crankiness, and he also describes his desired physical capabilities. Each sentiment is compared to an attribute of an animal in Jafta's country. Bold brown-and-white illustrations capture each emotion.

A Weekend with Wendell, Kevin Henkes, Greenwillow, 1986. Ages 5–7.
Sophie the mouse doesn't enjoy having Wendell as a weekend house guest. He is mischievous and overbearing. Morning to night, Wendell is a trial to Sophie and her parents. Just before he is about to leave, Sophie asserts herself and finds that they can have an equal friendship.

General

I Feel: A Picture Book of Emotions, George Ancona, Dutton, 1977. Ages 2–6.
Loneliness, happiness, and fear are among the emotions depicted with a single word, accompanied by black-and-white photographs. The inner feelings of children are captured in their faces and stances. For use with young children to identify displays of emotion or with older children as a game.

Embarrassment

A Birthday Bike for Brimhall, Judy Delton, Ill. by June Leary, Carolrhoda, 1985. Ages 4–8.
Brimhall Bear is too embarrassed to tell his friends that he doesn't know how to ride his new bike. He invents excuses to avoid riding it, while he secretly and unsuccessfully practices. Brimhall's abhorrence of the bike dissipates when he finds himself pedaling it to help his hurt friend.

Daniel's Duck, Clyde Bulla, Ill. by Joan Sandin, Harper, 1979. Ages 6–8. An I can read book.
Daniel labors all winter carving a wooden duck. He proudly displays it at the spring fair, only to find people laughing at it. Humiliated and angry, Daniel runs to throw the duck into the river. The famous local carver arrives to save the duck and teaches Daniel the value of his creation.

Generosity

I Know a Lady, Charlotte Zolotow, Ill. by James Stevenson, Greenwillow, 1984. Ages 4–8.
Sally describes an elderly woman who lives on her block. The lady gives the neighborhood children flowers from her garden and treats on holidays, and waves to them whenever they pass by. She is a gentle, generous person whom Sally has come to love. *Highly recommended.*

Wolf's Favor, Fulvio Testa, Dial Pr. Bks., 1986. Ages 4–8.
Porcupine seeks a favor from Wolf, asking him to open a nut. His hunger already satisfied, Wolf agrees to help. This spirit of generosity

spreads to others in the animal kingdom. One by one, strong animals do kindnesses for weaker ones. A beautifully illustrated fable for all ages.

Hatred

The Hating Book, Charlotte Zolotow, Ill. by Ben Shecter, Harper, 1969. Ages 5–8.

Despite insisting that she hates her friend, a young girl makes numerous attempts to gain the other child's attention. After continued encouragement from her mother, the girl confronts her friend to find out why she is being rejected. Together the children discover the misunderstanding that sabotaged their friendship.

Loneliness

Dear Phoebe, Sue Alexander, Ill. by Eileen Christelow, Little, 1984. Ages 4–8.

Phoebe Dormouse has grown up, and now it's time for her to find her own burrow. Once settled, she is lonely and misses her mother. Correspondence passes between the two, but Phoebe is not content until her mother reassures her that she is missed and loved.

Sadness

Are You Sad, Mama?, Elizabeth Winthrop, Ill. by Donna Diamond, Harper, 1979. O.P. Ages 4–7.

A little girl's mama is very sad, and nothing cheers her up. The child tries telling her a story, singing her a song, and drawing her a picture. Finally, a hug proves to be the answer for mama's happiness.

Security

Even If I Did Something Awful, Barbara Hazen, Ill. by Nancy Kincade, Atheneum, 1981. Ages 4–8.

A young girl seeks the reassurance of her mother's love by describing fantasized transgressions such as pinching the baby and lying. The mother promises her love, but the child will have to accept responsibility for her actions. When a real crime is revealed, the mother reassures her daughter, despite anger, that she will always love her. *Highly recommended*.

Selfishness

The Willow Maiden, Meghan Collins, Ill. by Laszlo Gal, Dial Pr. Bks., 1985. Ages 5–8.

Denis falls in love with Lisane, one of the Willow People, when she emerges from her tree. They may marry, but only if she returns to her tree in the spring. After an ecstatic winter, Denis concocts a plan to keep Lisane, but then he realizes that his selfishness will destroy her. Contains beautiful illustrations.

Shyness

Fiona's Bee, Beverly Keller, Ill. by Diane Paterson, Coward, 1975. O.P. Ages 5–7.

As shy Fiona waits longingly for new friends, she saves a bee from drowning. To her alarm, the bee climbs onto her shoulder. Fiona calmy walks to the park, hoping the bee will fly off. Along the way she gathers a following of intrigued children, eager to be her friends.

Greed

Birdsong, Gail E. Haley, Crown, 1984. Ages 5–8.

Jorinella, an old bird trapper, takes in an orphan named Birdsong when she envisions her potential monetary gain. As birds flock to hear Birdsong's piping, the greedy Jorinella uses her trickery to capture them. Birdsong realizes the deception and frees the birds, who in turn rescue her from Jorinella's wrath. Contains colorful illustrations.

The Crane Wife, Sumiko Yagawa, Tr. by Katherine Paterson, Ill. by Suekichi Akaba, Morrow, 1981. Ages 6–10.

After the peasant Yohei saves an injured crane, a beautiful woman appears, begging to be his wife. Impoverished, she weaves, but she warns Yohei not to watch. Yohei becomes greedy and asks his wife to weave again. Reluctantly, she agrees, but this time Yohei peeks. Horrified, Yohei sees his beloved become a crane again.

The Devil Take You, Barnabas Beane!, Mary B. Christian, Ill. by Anne Burgess, Crowell, 1980. O.P. Ages 5–8.

Selfish Barnabas Beane will share nothing with his neighbors. After he refuses shelter to Orphan John, Barnabas sees mysterious footprints. Fearing that the devil is coming for him, Barnabas seeks John's advice. John convinces him to reform his ways. The amusing cause of the footprints is never discovered by Barnabas.

It's Mine!, Leo Lionni, Knopf, 1985. Ages 4–8.

Three frogs, Milton, Rupert, and Lydia, quarrel continously about the water, earth, and air on their island. Tired of their endless shouts of "it's mine," a toad futilely urges them to stop. When a storm almost destroys the frogs, they learn the value of sharing. Accompanied by colorful, collage-style illustrations.

Ⓡ *Liang and the Magic Paintbrush*, Demi, Holt, 1980. O.P. Ages 5–10.

A Chinese boy, Liang, longs to paint, but he cannot afford a brush. In a dream, he is given a magic paintbrush that brings anything that is painted to life. The greedy emperor demands that Liang use the brush to fulfill his wishes, but the realities of the paintings finally destroy the emperor.

Little Sister and the Month Brothers, Retold by Beatrice S. deRegniers, Ill. by Margot Tomes, Clarion, 1976. Ages 5–8.

Trying to rid themselves of Little Sister, her stepmother and stepsister send her to the forest in January for violets and strawberries. The Month Brothers magically change the seasons just for Little Sister. Overcome by greed, her stepmother and stepsister seek more violets and strawberries but perish, leaving the farm to Little Sister. Contains humorous illustrations.

The Silver Cow: A Welsh Tale, Susan Cooper, Ill. by Warwick Hutton, Atheneum, 1983. Ages 5–9.

Mean Gwilyn sends his son, Huw, to watch the cows. There Huw is rewarded with a silver cow from the magic people for playing his harp. The cow brings Gwilyn wealth, but being greedy, he tries to butcher her. She returns to the lake, leaving Gwilyn in poverty.

Under the Shade of the Mulberry Tree, Demi Hitz, Prentice-Hall, 1979. O.P. Ages 4–7.

A rich man refuses to share the shade of his tree with a poor man, but he agrees to sell it. The poor man follows his shade wherever it goes, even into the house, bringing his animals with him. The greedy rich man realizes his foolish mistake and moves. A chinese folk tale with delicate illustrations.

Jealousy

Alex and the Baby, Mary Dickinson, Ill. by Charlotte Firmin, Andre Deutsch, 1982. Ages 3–7.

A story with surprising twists. Alex first rejects then happily entertains the family's new baby. However, soon it is revealed that the infant is not his sister; it is only temporarily being cared for by Alex's mother. The story ends happily with the parting of the intruder and a time to cuddle for mom and her big boy.

The Five Sparrows: A Japanese Folktale, adapted by Patricia M. Newton, Atheneum, 1982. Ages 5–8.

An old woman cares for a wounded sparrow despite mocking from her family and neighbors. The sparrow rewards her by returning with a seed that brings her wealth. When a jealous neighbor tries to emulate her, the consequences are disastrous. A whimsical look at the results of generosity and greed.

Happy Birthday, Crystal, Shirley Gordon, Ill. by Edward Frascino, Harper, 1981. O.P. Ages 5–8.

Because they do not live near each other, Susan has never been to Crystal's house. At Crystal's birthday party, Susan meets Crystal's other friend and neighbor. She must cope with her feelings of jealousy and with being an outsider. Despite her negative emotions, Susan behaves creditably and has fun.

His Mother's Dog, Liesel Skorpen, Ill. by M.E. Mullin, Harper, 1978. Ages 5–8.

When a young boy gets a dog for his birthday, he is disappointed that it prefers his mother's company. As time passes, it becomes obvious that his mother has the dog's loyalty, but he has its responsibility. The boy's resentment builds, but things change drastically with the arrival of a new sister.

Jealousy, Eva Eriksson, Carolrhoda, 1985. Ages 4–8.

Victor and Rosalie are best friends. When Rosalie gets the mumps, Victor plays with Sophie instead of grieving. Rosalie is jealous and tries to stop Sophie from competing for Victor's friendship. Both girls are miserable, but after trying to copy each other, Rosalie and Sophie laughingly discover that they can all be friends.

My Naughty Little Sister and Bad Harry's Rabbit, Dorothy Edwards, Ill. by Shirley Hughes, Prentice-Hall, 1981. Ages 4–7.

Naughty little sister and Bad Harry are friends, but their strong personalities cause conflict. When a picture of little sister, Rosey-Primrose, and Harry's rabbit appears in the newspaper, Harry becomes jealous because he was supposed to be included. All is forgiven when little sister retrieves the original photograph.

The Other Emily, Gibbs Davis, Ill. by Linda Shute, Houghton, 1984. Ages 5–8.

Emily is infatuated with her name and thinks it belongs only to her. The first day of school she is shocked and becomes angry and jealous when she learns that another child has the same name. Through the other Emily's patience and sharing, the two girls become friends.

Smile, Ernest and Celestine, Gabrielle Vincent, Greenwillow, 1982. Ages 4–8.

While tidying Ernest's room, Celestine discovers photographs of other mice with her friend. She is jealous and hurt because Ernest has no photos of her. Ernest remedies this by rushing off with her to a photographer. The text and illustrations capture the human foibles of Ernest, the bear, and Celestine, the mouse.

Stepdog, Marlene F. Shyer, Ill. by Judith Schermer, Scribner, 1983. Ages 5–8.

Terry is thrilled when her father marries Marilyn. But Hoover, Marilyn's dog, is jealous. He dunks Terry's stuffed animal in the lake, steals her hiking boots, and does other vindictive things. When Hoover is chained to the doghouse, Terry overcomes the stepdog's jealousy by rescuing him.

Two Is Company, Judy Delton, Ill. by Giulio Maestro, Crown, 1976. O.P. Ages 4–8.

Bear and Duck are two good friends. When Chipmunk moves into the neighborhood, Duck heartily welcomes her. Bear is disgruntled because he thinks Chipmunk is usurping Duck's friendship. But Chipmunk's generosity helps Bear overcome his jealousy.

The Wonderful Mrs. Trumbly, Sally Wittman, Ill. by Margot Apple, Harper, 1982. Ages 5–8.

Martin loves his new teacher, Mrs. Trumbly, despite his classmates' teasing. Their friendship is marred only when Mr. Klein, the music teacher, becomes her suitor. Unable to combat the courtship, Martin finally overcomes his jealousy when he realizes that Mrs. Trumbly wants to continue their special friendsip. *Highly recommended*.

Joy

Guess Who My Favorite Person Is, Byrd Baylor, Ill. by Robert A. Parker, Scribner, 1977. Ages 6–9.

A young girl and a man meet in an alfalfa field and spend the afternoon telling each other about their favorite things. Some of hers are the color brown and wind on her face. His favorites include falling stars and freshly baked bread. A sensual exploration of life's simple joys.

Someday, Said Mitchell, Barbara Williams, Ill. by Kay Chorao, 1976. O.P. Ages 4–7.

Each time Mitchell tells his mother what he will buy to help her when he's bigger, she responds with a request for his help. Mitchell dreams of having more time for them to relax together. Gently, his mother shows him that they have time now to share the joy they find in each other.

Love

Good Dog, Bad Dog, Corinne Gerson, Ill. by Emily A. McCully, Atheneum, 1983. Ages 5–8.

Tim worries about his dog, Misty, who is rambunctious yet loving with the family. Misty even saves Tim's life, but with outsiders she growls and snaps. After Misty bites a policeman, Tim resolves to discipline her, but realizes he will still love her even if she cannot behave.

Grandma's House, Elaine Moore, Ill. by Elise Primavera, Lothrop, 1985. Ages 5–8.

A girl draws a parallel between her summer visit and Grandma's garden. Each begins with strawberries and ends with plums. After wildlife have eaten her fruit all season, Grandma finally warns the squirrels to leave her plum trees alone. At that time, the child realizes that her loving relationship with Grandma is more important than the harvest of the fruit. *Highly recommended*.

Grandpa and Bo, Kevin Henkes, Greenwillow, 1986. Ages 4–7.

Bo visits his Grandpa for the summer. They spend their time fishing, playing, and enjoying nature. They regret not being able to spend Christmas together, so they celebrate the holiday during the summer. As the visit comes to a close, Grandpa and Bo share a wish on a falling star.

Hug Me, Patti Stren, Harper, 1977. Ages 4–8.

Elliot Kravitz is a porcupine searching for affection. His other porcupine friends love having quills that keep others away, but Elliot longs for a friend to love him. Hugging objects proves to be unsatisfactory. At last, Elliot finds such a friend and discovers that hugging is truly wonderful. *Highly recommended*.

I Love My Mother, Paul Zindel, Ill. by John Melo, Harper, 1975. Ages 4–8.

A young boy describes his mother, who teaches him judo and soothes away nightmares. She saves him the last french fry and tells him to have fun when he decides to run away. When he misses his father, she says that his father misses him, too. Illustrations reflect the mother's and son's loving exuberance.

I Love You Mouse, John Graham, Ill. by Tomie de Paola, Harcourt, 1976. Ages 3–7.

A young boy imagines all the things he would do if he were the parent of various animals. For each he would provide shelter and share in their favorite pastimes. This tender story ends with the child's father describing how his own love as a parent is manifested. Endearing illustrations.

Jafta's Mother, Hugh Lewin, Ill. by Lisa Kopper, Carolrhoda, 1983. Ages 3–7.

Jafta, a young African boy, lovingly describes his mother, comparing her to the familiar things in his world. She is like the earth, brown and strong, and like the sun, waking him each day. Although she occasionally storms, Jafta's mother, like the sky, is always there. *Highly recommended.*

Little Gorilla, Ruth Bornstein, Houghton, 1976. Ages 2–6.

Little Gorilla is loved by his family and by the other animals in the jungle. They care for him and are there when needed. Then Little Gorilla grows big. Forlorn-looking, Little Gorilla is reassured that despite his size, everyone still loves him. A storytime favorite that captivates even the youngest listeners.

May I Visit?, Charlotte Zolotow, Ill. by Erik Blegvad, Harper, 1976. O.P. Ages 4–8.

Following her married sister's visit, a girl speculates about visiting home when she's grown. She promises not to commit misdemeanors. Mother assures the child that even if she knocks over the plants or tracks in mud, it will be fun to have her, just as it is now. For children who think their parents' love is conditional.

Mother, Mother, I Want Another, Maria Polushkin, Ill. by Diane Dawson, Crown, 1978. Ages 2–6.

Mrs. Mouse is dismayed when her baby requests another mother at bedtime. She fetches Mrs. Duck, but Baby Mouse still wants another. One animal mother after another is unacceptable until Baby explains that he wants another kiss, not another mother. A humorous, endearing story that delights storytime listeners.

Owly, Mike Thaler, Ill. by David Wiesner, Harper, 1982. Ages 3–7.

Owly, the little owl, has endless questions for his mother. The ocean with its waves and the sky filled with stars arouse his curiosity. His mother encourages him to find the answers, and her wisdom also helps him to understand the depth of their love for each other.

Peabody, Rosemary Wells, Dial Pr. Bks., 1983. Ages 3–8.

Peabody, the teddy bear, is Annie's birthday present. They are inseparable until Rita, the walking-talking doll, arrives on Annie's next birthday. Annie neglects Peabody, but Robert, her brother, inadvertently restores things to normal. When Robert ruins Rita by bathing her, Peabody returns to Annie's affection. Hilarious illustrations accompany this endearing story. *Highly recommended.*

Say It!, Charlotte Zolotow, Ill. by James Stevenson, Greenwillow, 1980. Ages 5–8.

As a little girl and her mother go for a walk on an autumn day, the child keeps urging her mother to "say it." The mother's responses are not adequate. At last, the mother tells the child that she loves her, and that is exactly what the girl has wanted to hear all along. *Highly recommended*.

Thistle, Walter Wangerin, Jr., Ill. by Marcia Sewall, Harper, 1983. Ages 7–9.

Thistle is the youngest child of a potato farmer and his wife. She is plain and loving; while her brothers and sister are attractive and vain. When Pudge, the potato monster, devours their parents, all the children except Thistle reject the help of a disgustingly ugly witch, who saves the family. An allegorical tale.

The Velveteen Rabbit, Margery Williams, Ill. by William Nicholson, Doubleday, 1958; Ill. by Michael Hague, Holt, 1983. Ages 5 + .

Skin Horse explains to the Velveteen Rabbit what it means to be real. But until Rabbit is taken off the nursery shelf and becomes the inseparable companion of the boy, he does not understand. As Rabbit gets worn, he experiences the magic of love that makes him real. A timeless classic about the power of love.

When I Was Little, Lyn L. Hoopes, Ill. by Marcia Sewall, Dutton, 1983. Ages 5–8.

A young girl goes skating with her mother, who is carrying baby brother Billy in her arms. As they walk through the snow and then skate, the child questions her parents' love. Gently, her mother reassures the girl that she is loved more with each passing day.

The Wild Swans, Hans Christian Andersen, retold by Amy Ehrlich, Ill. by Susan Jeffers, Dial, 1981. Ages 6 + .

Elise's love for her eleven brothers is a stronger power than the hatred of their stepmother. When the young princes are transformed into swans, their sister endures great hardship to save them. A beautifully illustrated classic for all ages.

Serenity

All Alone, Kevin Henkes, Greenwillow, 1981. Ages 5–8.

A young boy describes his satisfaction with being alone sometimes. When alone, he is more aware of nature, can ponder life, and can pretend. As his reflection ends, he contemplates what his friends are doing. The book's gentle illustrations reflect the boy's contentment.

Dawn, Uri Shulevitz, Farrar, 1974. Ages 3 + .

An old man and his grandson sleep by the lake in the stillness of the night. Slowly, signs of a new day awaken them, and they row to the middle of the lake to experience the dazzling dawn. The text's few words and stunning illustrations exemplify serenity.

Fog Drift Morning, Deborah K. Ray, Harper, 1983. Ages 5–8.

In the stillness of the misty dawn, a girl and her mother go to pick blueberries. The young narrator creates a tranquil mood in a framework of nature by describing their walk near the ocean and hills. The child and her mother delight in each other during this quiet time and return home to a bright new morning. Contains lovely illustrations.

Karin's Christmas Walk, Susan Pearson, Ill. by Trinka H. Noble, Dial, 1980. Ages 5–8.

Karin is worried that Uncle Jerry won't arrive for Christmas. As she walks to the store for her mother, Karin reminisces about their shared times. Before she gets home, Karin sees Uncle Jerry's truck in the driveway. Karin pauses and savors her anticipation of the most wonderful time of the year. *Highly recommended.*

Katie in the Morning, Crescent Dragonwagon, Ill. by Betsy Day, Harper, 1983. Ages 4–7.

Before the sun is fully up, Katie rises to claim the day. The silent joys of nature are hers to relish before the others awaken. Katie is enthralled by her surroundings as she walks to buy the morning paper. She returns to her family of "night owls," who are in awe of their "early bird."

Right Now, David Kherdian, Ill. by Nonny Hogrogian, Knopf, 1983. Ages 4–8.

A young girl reflects on the many happenings in her short life, some happy and exhilarating, others sad and painful. Each thought of a past or future experience is countered with her pleasure in the present. Best of all, she is satisfied with herself and with her current situation.

® *When I Was Young in the Mountains*, Cynthia Rylant, Ill. by Diane Goode, Dutton, 1982. Ages 4–8.

A young girl describes her childhood experiences with her grandparents. The story presents a picture of total contentment resulting from the girl's delight in such simple pleasures as baths in front of the stove and a dip in the muddy swimming hole. Winsome yet humorous illustrations capture the folksy mood of the reminiscences.

Related Titles

Anger

Wheels, Jane R. Thomas.

Expressing Feelings

Frankie Is Staying Back, Ron Roy.

General

Loneliness

Aaron's Door, Miska Miles.

Waiting, Nicki Weiss.

Shyness

Superduper Teddy, Johanna Hurwitz.

Jealousy

Henrietta and the Gong from Hong Kong, Winifred Rosen.

Much Bigger than Martin, Steven Kellogg.

Princess Pearl, Nicki Weiss.

Love

Will It Be Okay?, Crescent Dragonwagon.

Chapter 6

Family

General

Adoption
Divorce
Foster Care
Grandparents

Parents Working/Not Working
Remarriage and Stepfamilies
Separation
Sibling Rivalry

The concept of family encompasses every human being in all societies and cultures. The life cycle of each person evolves within the family context from birth to death. It is an ongoing process that overlaps the generations: one member dies; others marry, give birth, or adopt; and the family goes on.

There seems to be a predictable pattern as families move through their stages of growth. In fact, a family's structure becomes more complex as it changes in form and function over the years. The configuration of a family is more variable than ever before. Consequently, the image of the modern family lacks the sense of stability known to past generations. This perception exists for several reasons. Families are more mobile, and often both parents work outside the home. There are increasing numbers of divorces, remarriages, and blended families. Unlike earlier generations, grandparents frequently don't live with the immediate family. Sometimes they are not wanted. Often, grandparents choose to remain independent and stay in their own homes or move into nursing homes.

However, changes in society, and in the more traditional sense of family, do not alter the vital and basic role of family life. It remains the nurturing center for human development and is the source of physical and emotional health for its members. It is in this milieu that children are socialized, transformed from helpless infants into responsible members of society.

Just as children are the leaders of our future, the time will come when they will be adults caring for new family members. Growing up is difficult, even in the least stressful environment, but instability and changes in the family constellation easily overwhelm children. All children have unique individual stories about family life, but their worries and concerns about their relationship with family members are universal. From children's frame of reference, the arrival of a new brother or sister may threaten their position in the family. Divorce also brings universal anxieties, guilt, confusion, misconceptions, and fears of abandonment. Placement in a foster family is particularly difficult for children. At any age, emotional problems can surface, such as the questioning of self-identity when children learn that they are adopted, or the oldest sibling's coming to terms with birth order factors such as setting a good example and sharing.

Regardless of the specific issue, children may experience difficulty in coping with alterations in family life. They approach the situation in a simplistic, often innocent manner and are cognitively capable of understanding something only as being good or bad. Often they accept responsibility for the bad and do not have the skill to deal independently with certain circumstances realistically.

If left alone to face these difficulties, children lose their ability to depend on the family as a source of strength and comfort. By finding love and understanding in the intimate warmth of family members, they can confidently follow their journey of self-discovery and fulfillment.

As problems and changes related to the family arise, adults need to be honest with children, as in the case of adoption or divorce. It is imperative that children be helped to deal with questions in their own simple terms. They need to hear the truth, even though it may be painful. At other times, parents may need to confront a child's negative behavior and to encourage the recognition of negative feelings, as in the case of sibling rivalry. Often, children require help sorting out conflicting emotions. Ignoring a child's internal conflicts over family issues can lead to lifelong identity and adjustment problems.

Parents and other caregivers can help children deal with family stress in a healthy manner through an open and accepting attitude, role modeling, and discussion. All of these techniques can be facilitated through the use of books with children. Books can encourage children to express their thoughts and feelings, demonstrate positive ways of handling difficulties, and expose children to other lifestyles.

Although each child's situation is unique, there are recurring themes common to all children. As books answer questions about such topics as divorce, adoption, and grandparents' aging, children learn to deal with a multitude of feelings that are not easy to articulate. Books can aid in the expression of feelings and in the acknowledgment of expectations that accompany significant family events. Stories can provide a catharsis for children and help them understand that they are not alone in their experience. For example, many children suffer from jealousy at the arrival of a new sibling or struggle with the realization of a parent's imperfections. Books can help children to come to terms with family problems and to continue the process of growing up.

Books can be a shared experience between caregivers and children at any age and provide a bond between the reader and listener. They can be a mechanism to demonstrate the adult's understanding of the child's personal needs and to facilitate discussion of the child's concern. There are a variety of books relevant to each child's circumstances.

An abundance of books on families is available. Many on relationships are excellent but do not deal with problems. The best problem-oriented books are included here.

General

Family Relationships

All Kinds of Families, Norma Simon, Ill. by Joe Lasker, Albert Whitman, 1976. Ages 5–8.

This book explains that despite differences, all families have common characteristics. They share good and bad times and grow together. Parents, children, and other relatives are a family, whether together or apart. They may not always get along, but they try to care for each other. This book defines the sense of belonging in a family.

Families, Meredith Tax, Ill. by Marylin Hafner, Little, 1981. Ages 4–7.

Six-year-old Angie explains what comprises a family. She lives with her mother in New York and during vacations, with her father in Boston. Angie's friends live with single parents, and with extended and blended families. This informational picture book stresses that families vary in composition, but they all share one important characteristic—love.

A Gift for Mama, Esther Hautzig, Ill. by Donna Diamond, Viking, 1981. Ages 7–12.

Sara is determined to buy Mama a present, but she faces breaking the family tradition of creating homemade gifts. She secretly takes in mending in order to earn money to buy slippers. On Mother's Day, Mama seems disappointed with the surprise until she understands the diligence and love that made it possible. *Highly recommended*.

Good as New, Barbara Douglass, Ill. by Patience Brewster, Lothrop, 1982. Ages 4–7.

Grady reluctantly allows his screaming cousin to play with his teddy bear. The abused bear looks awful when returned, but Grandpa promises to fix it. Grady has doubts, but the result is a bear that's better than new. Subsequently, Grandpa, Grady, and Bear leave the house whenever the cousin visits.

Harry's Mom, Barbara A. Porte, Ill. by Yossi Abolafia, Greenwillow, 1985. Ages 6–8. Greenwillow Read-alone.

Harry reads the dictionary's definition of an orphan and decides that he is one since his mother is dead. His father reminds him that all his relatives love him and tells Harry about his adventurous mother. Harry decides that he will be like his mother and, of course, like his dad too.

Here I Am, an Only Child, Marlene F. Shyer, Ill. by Donald Carrick, Scribner, 1985. Ages 5–8.

Being an only child can be both bad and good. A boy envisions sharing nighttime whispers and dividing the chores with siblings. However, he always gets Dad's lap and doesn't have to fight to watch his favorite television programs. As an only child, it's always his turn, even for a dental checkup.

Seven Kisses in a Row, Patricia MacLachlan, Ill. by Maria P. Marrella, Harper, 1983. Ages 7–11.

Aunt Evelyn and Uncle Eliot stay with Emma and Zachary while their parents are away. However, the aunt and uncle have too many rules, and Emma misses getting seven kisses in a row from her parents. After their bad beginning, Emma teaches her relatives flexibility and parenting, and develops an appreciation for their uniqueness.

That New Pet!, Alane Ferguson, Ill. by Catherine Stock, Lothrop, 1986. Ages 4–7.

A parrot, dog, and cat have their comfortable existence disrupted by the appearance of a new "pet." The stranger, a baby, captivates all her parents' attention. The pets' schemes to be rid of her fail miserably. Jealousy turns to loving acceptance when they discover their power to soothe the infant.

Whatever Happened to Beverly Bigler's Birthday?, Barbara Williams, Ill. by Emily McCully, Harcourt, 1979. Ages 5–8.

It's Beverly's birthday, but no one seems to care because it's also her sister's wedding day. A forlorn Beverly messes up her dress, spills the rice, and nearly destroys the wedding cake while searching for her birthday cake. Finally giving up, Beverly finds a surprise party waiting for her.

Your Family, My Family, Joan Drescher, Walker, 1980. Ages 4–8.

An informative fiction book about families. A family can be large or small; the composition varies depending on who is in each family. However, it's the togetherness, sharing, and love that makes a family. A good introduction to the concept of family.

Multiple Births

My Three Uncles, Yossi Abolafia, Greenwillow, 1985. Ages 5–8.

A girl has uncles who are identical triplets. They don't seem to make much effort to help others tell them apart. Finally, one uncle, Max, shares with his niece the secret of identifying each one. The girl learns how to tell them apart by their individual idiosyncracies.

The Triplets, Barbara Seuling, Clarion, 1980. Ages 5–8.

Triplets Mattie, Hattie, and Patty are frustrated because everyone keeps mixing them up. None of the girls get credit for her own accomplishments. In defense, they lock themselves in their room, refusing all requests to come out. The combined ingenuity of their offenders restores their separate identities. For all identical siblings.

Parents' Imperfections

Ⓡ *Daddy Is a Monster...Sometimes*, John Steptoe, Lippincott, 1980. Ages 5–8.

Daddy is perceived as a monster when he refuses to buy Bweela and Javaka an ice cream cone after they've already had one. He also becomes a monster when they play with their food while eating. When questioned, Daddy tells Bweela and Javaka that he becomes a monster at times because they are sometimes monster children.

The Handsomest Father, Deborah Hautzig, Ill. by Muriel Batherman, Greenwillow, 1979. O.P. Ages 6–8.

Marsha's classmate, Kathryn, has proclaimed her own father the handsomest man. Marsha therefore dreads Fathers' Visiting Day, aware of the possibility that she might be embarrassed by her own father. After his honking sneeze, Marsha's father shines; and by the end of the story, Marsha declares her balding father the handsomest one present. For children struggling with parents' imperfections.

I Wish Laura's Mommy Was My Mommy, Barbara Power, Ill. by Marylin Hafner, Lippincott, 1979. Ages 6–7. I-like-to-read book.

Jennifer is thrilled that Laura's mommy will babysit her and her brothers when Mother gets a job. At Laura's, snacks include donuts, and the girls have no responsibilities. After a week, however, the girls must help out at Laura's. Jennifer has special times with her own mother and no longer wishes that Laura's mommy were hers.

The Kid with the Red Suspenders, LouAnn Gaeddert, Ill. by Mary B. Schwark, Dutton, 1983. Ages 7–9.

Rob, the new boy at school, taunts Hamilton by calling him "Mommy's little lamb." Hamilton makes devious but futile attempts to show he is not. Only after Hamilton cuts school with Rob does his mother begin to realize his difficulties and relax her hold on Hamilton.

My Daddy Is Really Something, Lois Osborn, Ill. by Rodney Pate, Albert Whitman, 1983. Ages 6–8.

Every time Harry George tells something good about his father, his friend, Ron, diminishes it with a story about his own father's greatness. When Harry George learns that Ron's father is dead, he is angry about Ron's lies but glad that his own father is real. Helpful in appreciating the inadequacies of a parent.

Problems at Home

The Do-Something Day, Joe Lasker, Viking, 1982. Ages 5–8.

No one in Bernie's family needs him, so he runs away. Some shop owners ask for his help and reward his service. By evening, a satisfied Bernie eagerly goes home to share his earnings with his family. Grateful for the gift, his mother reminds Bernie that the family's greatest need is to love him.

Saturday I Ran Away, Susan Pearson, Ill. by Susan Jeschke, Lippincott, 1981. O.P. Ages 5–8.

Emily's sister and brother blame and ostracize her, Mom sets boundaries, and Dad shoos her from the bathroom. Running away is the perfect solution, but Emily discovers that the entire family has the same desire. When Emily ingeniously brings the family together for a day of escape, they learn a lesson in caring.

Something Is Wrong at My House, Diane Davis, Ill. by Marina Megale, Parenting Pr., 1984. Ages 5–9.

A boy describes the anguish of living with domestic violence. He experiences the pain and sense of helplessness common to children in similar situations, yet he discovers ways to care for himself and find help. Two texts allow use of this book with preschool- and school-aged children.

Sometimes Mama and Papa Fight, Marjorie W. Sharmat, Ill. by Kay Chorao, Harper, 1980. Ages 4–7.

Kevin and Millicent hate their parents' fights. Usually Mama and Papa are happy and loving, but now they are shouting. Kevin thinks of ways to stop the fight, but before he can take action, Mama and Papa come to tell him that their fight is over. A good introduction to the concept that arguments can be normal.

Sometimes My Mom Drinks Too Much, Kevin Kenny and Helen Krull, Ill. by Helen Cogancherry, Raintree, 1980. Ages 5–9.

Maureen is confused and embarrassed by her mother's erratic behavior. When a friend asks her if her mother is drunk, Maureen questions her dad. He explains mom's alcoholism, but he does not intervene until mom and her boss decide she needs treatment. Simplistic, but an adequate introduction to a devastating problem.

What's "Drunk," Mama?, Al-Anon Family Group Headquarters, Inc., 1977. Ages 6–10.

Christy is angry that her daddy is always sick from drinking and that her mama is either crying or mad. Her world is filled with unkept promises and worry. Through Al-Anon, Christy's family starts a gradual recovery and learns the importance of caring for themselves. An optimstic yet realistic approach.

When Can Daddy Come Home?, Martha W. Hickman, Ill. by Frances Livingston, Abingdon, 1983. Ages 5–8.

Anderson's family moves to a new town to be near his father, who is in prison. He dreads the new school, fearing he will be ostracized. When Anderson reaches out in compassion to another child, he gains a friend and resolves some of his own ambivalent feelings toward his father.

Sibling Relationships

Brother Mouky and the Falling Sun, Karen Whiteside, Harper, 1980. Ages 6–9.

In rhythmic black English, Mouky broods about his anger at his brother. True to his mother's teachings, Mouky knows that he cannot be angry when the sun goes down. His pleas to the environment for help go unanswered until Mouky understands that forgiveness is within himself.

More Stories Julian Tells, Ann Cameron, Ill. by Ann Strugnell, Knopf, 1986. Ages 6–9.

Five stories about Julian, his best friend, Gloria, and his younger brother, Huey. One story on the responsibilities of an older sibling warrants recommendation. Julian and Gloria ostracize Huey because he is fearful of their game. In trying to prove his bravery, Huey hurts himself, and Julian learns a lesson in caring.

My Sister Celia, Judith Caseley, Greenwillow, 1986. Ages 4–8.
Celia is much older than her sister, Emma. Once a week they spend time together doing things that become traditions. Suddenly Emma's secure relationship with her sister appears shattered when Celia decides to marry Ben. Calling upon their traditions, the bride proves to Emma that they will always be close. A special approach to this unique problem.

The Oldest Kid, Elaine Knox-Wagner, Ill. by Gail Owens, Albert Whitman, 1981. Ages 5–8.
A young girl describes her position as the oldest child in the family. Setting a good example, being polite, and being responsible seem to be burdens. At a family picnic, she complains to her grandfather about the unfairness of her role, but discovers that being the oldest can bring privileges, too.

On the Way to the Movies, Charlotte Herman, Ill. by Diane Dawson, Dutton, 1980. O.P. Ages 5–8.
Simon is sure that his younger brother, Freddie, will be scared at the monster movie, but Freddie says he won't. On the way there, Freddie tries Simon's patience beyond belief. While waiting in line, Simon is the one who becomes frightened in hearing about the horror of the movie. A humorous role reversal transpires.

Sisters, David McPhail, Harcourt, 1984. Ages 4–8.
Two sisters are different but also share favorite things. One loves colored socks and sleeping late. The other prefers being barefoot and rising at dawn. Together they enjoy baking cookies and dancing. Despite their contrasts and conflicts, they love each other. A fine portrayal of the special bond between siblings. *Highly recommended*.

You'll Soon Grow into Them, Titch, Pat Hutchins, Greenwillow, 1983. Ages 3–6.
As the youngest child, Titch gets his brother's and sister's outgrown clothing, which doesn't really fit him. With the arrival of a new sibling, his parents take Titch shopping. Titch presents his old clothes to his new baby brother, saying "he'll soon grow into them." For any child who must wear his or her siblings' castoffs.

Adoption

Aaron's Door, Miska Miles, Ill. by Alan E. Cober, Little, 1977. O.P. Ages 6–10.
After his parents' desertion, Aaron cannot trust anyone. A couple

adopts Aaron and his sister, but Aaron locks his bedroom door against them. The couple pleads for two days, then the man breaks down the door. Finding a place for himself at the table, Aaron realizes that he is wanted. Vivid illustrations capture Aaron's loneliness. *Highly recommended.*

Abby, Jeannette Caines, Ill. by Steven Kellogg, Harper, 1973. Ages 4–7.

Abby loves discussing her adoption with her family. When she begs her brother to read her baby book, he is rushed and tells her he doesn't like her because she's a girl. Upset, Abby retaliates. Finally, Kevin admits that he's proud of Abby. A warm-hearted depiction of affection between siblings. *Highly recommended.*

The Adopted One: An Open Family Book for Parents and Children Together, Sara B. Stein, photographs by Erika Stone, Walker, 1979. O.P. Ages 3–8.

Joshua feels excluded at a family gathering. He questions his mother about his adoption but is not completely satisfied with her answer. After receiving criticism from relatives, Joshua shouts at his parents. Their response gives Joshua the reassurance he is seeking. Accompanied by an insightful parent text on the mixed feelings experienced by an adopted child.

Adoption Is for Always, Linda W. Girard, Ill. by Judith Friedman, Albert Whitman, 1986. Ages 5–8.

Celia finally assimilates what her parents have always told her: she is adopted. The realization leaves her angry and confused. Her mother, father, and teacher help her understand that she was a good baby and that her birth parents loved her. Reassured, Celia rejoices that she will always belong to her adoptive parents.

The Boy Who Wanted a Family, Shirley Gordon, Ill. by Charles Robinson, Harper, 1980. Ages 6–9.

Once before, Michael was almost adopted. Now Miss Graham wants to adopt him, but the adoption won't be legal for a year. Despite anxious moments, Michael develops a sense of belonging by the time the judge approves the adoption.

The Foundling Fox, Irina Korschunow, Tr. by James Skofield from German, Ill. by Reinhard Michl, Harper, 1982. Ages 5–8.

When a vixen provides warmth and food for an orphaned fox, she cannot bear to leave it. After the vixen protects the foundling from hostile animals and from the malicious criticism of a neighbor, she is unable to distinguish the foundling from her other kits. An allegory about the love of an adoptive mother.

I Am Adopted, Susan Lapsley, Ill. by Michael Charlton, Bodley Head, 1983. Ages 2¹/₂–6.

Charles and his sister, Sophie, are adopted. Charles describes simply his life with his special friend and family. Most important, Charles explains that "adoption means belonging."

Is That Your Sister?: A True Story of Adoption, Catherine and Sherry Bunin, Pantheon, 1976. O.P. Ages 6–9.

In the straightforward manner of a six-year-old, Catherine discusses what adoption means. She and her younger sister are adopted and are racially different from their parents and brothers. Catherine warmly reveals their story starting from the adoption process through becoming a family.

The Mulberry Bird: Story of an Adoption, Ann B. Brodzinsky, Ill. by Diana L. Stanley, Perspectives Pr., 1986. Ages 6–9.

Mother bird struggles valiantly to feed and protect her baby, until a storm destroys the nest. After the mother's attempts to care for her child prove futile, Wise Owl solves the heartbreaking dilemma by facilitating the baby bird's adoption. A tale that can aid children in understanding why their birth parents have given them up for adoption.

Poor Boy, Rich Boy, Clyde R. Bulla, Ill. by Marcia Sewall, Harper, 1982. Ages 6–8. An I can read book.

Uncle Paul is overjoyed to find his orphaned nephew, Coco. He strives to give the boy anything money can buy, but he fails to realize Coco's basic desire for love. Only after Uncle Paul frees a captured horse at Coco's request does the uncle come to understand that he and Coco need only each other.

Somebody Else's Child, Roberta Silman, Ill. by Chris Conover, Warne, 1976. Ages 7–11.

Peter's special friendship with Puddin' Paint, his school bus driver, is tainted by a comment on adoption. Peter is hurt and questions his own adoption. When Peter joins the frantic search for Puddin' Paint's cherished dogs, the two come to understand how a sense of loving and caring develops in relationships. *Highly recommended*.

We Don't Look like Our Mom and Dad, Harriett L. Sobol, photographs by Patricia Agre, Coward, 1984. Ages 7–12.

Eric, age ten, and Joshua, age eleven, are adopted Korean-born children. Busy with school, sports, and music, the boys rarely think of their heritage, but their parents keep it alive for them. No one is biologically related, but they are a family because of their love and sharing. A nonfiction photo-essay.

"Why Was I Adopted?", Carole Livingston, Ill. by Arthur Robins, Stuart, 1978. Ages 6–8.

An informational book that answers questions on adoption. In a direct, honest manner, the text explains how everyone is unique yet special, the difference between birth parents and adoptive parents, and the significance of adoption. A good introduction to the subject of adoption, that stresses the loving bond that develops between parents and children.

Divorce

Always, Always, Crescent Dragonwagon, Ill. by Arieh Zeldich, Macmillan, 1984. Ages 5–8.

During the school year, a young girl lives with her mother in New York; summers are spent in her father's Colorado cabin. She ponders the differences of life with each as her thoughts wander from take-out Chinese food to firewood kindling. She has absolute certainty that both parents will always love her. Illustrations capture the girl's reflective mood. *Highly recommended*.

Daddy, Jeannette Caines, Ill. by Ronald Himler, Harper, 1977. Ages 4–8.

Windy's parents are divorced. She shares each Saturday with her father in silly, fun-loving ways. Daddy lives with a woman named Paula, who joins in some of the antics. Windy worries about him when she and Daddy are apart, but her concern is banished each new Saturday. *Highly recommended*.

Davey Come Home, Margaret Teibl, Ill. by Jacqueline B. Smith, Harper, 1979. Ages 7–10.

Davey's father has custody of him, but after school there's a babysitter. Davey is never made to come home for supper, which to him represents the epitome of being loved. When irresponsible teenager Jodie is replaced by Mrs. Summers, Davey thrives in her care but fears she will leave. When tested, Mrs. Summers does make Davey come home.

Dinosaurs Divorce: A Guide for Changing Families, Laurene K. Brown and Marc Brown, Atlantic Monthly Pr., 1986. Ages 4–7.

Caricatures of dinosaurs in comic book format accompany the text, which explains divorce to children. Emotions are explored as well as the adjustment to having two homes and stepfamilies. The humorous illustrations do not detract from the seriousness of the subject, and the animal figures may be less threatening for children than real-life characters. *Highly recommended*.

I Have Two Families, Doris W. Helmering, Ill. by Heidi Palmer, Abingdon, 1981. Ages 6–8.

Eight-year-old Patty describes how her parents arrived at a custody arrangement and how it affects their lives. In a matter-of-fact manner, Patty explains the routines she and her brother follow with each parent. The book is somewhat simplistic about the ease of adjustment but provides a good introduction to divorce.

Mom and Dad Don't Live Together Any More, Kathy Stinson, Ill. by Nancy L. Reynolds, Annick Pr., 1985. Ages 3–5.

A preschool girl describes her life since her parents' divorce. Although she wishes they were together, she shares special times with each. Mommy puts barrettes in her hair, and Daddy carries her on his shoulders. Gradually, she accepts that she has the love of both, even though they are not together.

Mommy and Daddy Are Divorced, Patricia Perry and Mariette Lynch, Dial Pr. Bks., 1978. Ages 4–8.

Ned tells what life is like for him and his brother, Joey, since their parents' recent divorce. The preschool boys react to their new situation with conflicting emotions and gradual acceptance. A straightforward, reassuring treatment of how some children respond to their parents' divorce, accompanied by black-and-white photos.

One More Time, Louis Baum, Ill. by Paddy Bouma, Morrow, 1986. Ages 4–7.

Simon and his dad share Sunday in the city. As they play in the park, then have a picnic on the train home, Simon often requests "one more time." Dad and Simon easily say good-bye because they know that they'll see each other again soon. Colorful illustrations reflect the love shared by a boy and his noncustodial father.

Two Homes to Live In: A Child's-Eye View of Divorce, Barbara S. Hazen, Ill. by Peggy Luks, 1978. Ages 4–8.

Niki's parents are divorced. She worries that the divorce might have been her fault, but her parents reassure her that it is their problem and that they will always love her. In time, Niki accepts the finality of the situation and learns what it means to have divorced parents and two homes.

Two Special Cards, Sonia O. Lisker and Leigh Dean, Ill. by Sonia O. Lisker, Harcourt, 1976. O.P. Ages 5–8.

Despite their arguing, Hazel does not want her parents to get a divorce. Gradually, as she and her brother experience life with each of their parents apart, she accepts their new reality. When her search for divorce cards proves futile, Hazel makes one for each of her parents to show them her love.

What Would You Do? A Child's Book about Divorce, Barbara S. Cain and Elissa P. Benedek, Ill. by James Cummins, Saturday Evening Post, 1976. O.P. Ages 4–7.
A nonfiction book that asks children how they would react to their parents' fighting, divorcing, and deciding custody arrangements. Issues of readjustment, both negative and positive, are also addressed. Common responses of children are included to answer the questions raised here. The format of the book is conducive to helping children express their own feelings.

Foster Care

Foster Child, Loretta Holz, Messner, 1984. Ages 7–10.
Peter lives with a foster family while his mother is being treated for alcoholism. He has never had siblings; now Peter has two sisters and a brother. His foster parents have many rules to which Peter must adjust. Although he is happy, he hopes he will soon return home. Nonfiction. *Highly recommended*.

Mama One, Mama Two, Patricia MacLachlan, Ill. by Ruth L. Bornstein, Harper, 1982. Ages 5–8.
Because of her depression, Mama One, Maudie's mother, is unable to care for her, so Maudie comes to live with Katherine, her foster mother. During the baby's nighttime feeding, Katherine and Maudie tell a story of hardship and love. Warm illustrations reflect Katherine's solicitude and Maudie's anticipation of Mama One's return.

My Little Foster Sister, Muriel Stanek, Ill. by Judith Cheng, Albert Whitman, 1981. Ages 5–7.
Penny, a foster child, comes to stay with a young girl's family. The narrator, an only child, jealously guards her rights against the interloper. When a bully dominates Penny, Penny and the girl's friendship begins. Parting is difficult for both girls when Penny leaves to be adopted. A somewhat contrived story but an adequate introduction to foster care.

Grandparents

Alzheimer's Disease

Grandma Didn't Wave Back, Rose Blue, Ill. by Ted Lewin, Watts, 1972. Ages 7–11.
To Debbie, Grandma means delicious food, beautiful shawls, and

warm talks after school. Now, however, Grandma doesn't get dressed and forgets things. Debbie rebels when putting Grandma in a nursing home is discussed, but she becomes resigned after Grandma wanders outside in her nightgown. A helpful tale for families of patients with Alzheimer's disease, even though grandma is incorrectly labeled "senile." *Highly recommended*.

Grandpa Doesn't Know It's Me, Donna Guthrie, Ill. by Katy K. Arnsteen, Human Sci. Pr., 1986. Ages 5–8.

When Grandpa's forgetfulness becomes dangerous, he moves in with Lizzie's family. They patiently strive to keep him active and safe. Lizzie describes her fears of Alzheimer's disease, the unpleasantness of being accused of theft by Grandpa, and the anguish of not being recognized. A compassionate portrayal, that is helpful in understanding Alzheimer's disease.

My Grandma's in a Nursing Home, Judy Delton and Dorothy Tucker, Ill. by Charles Robinson, Albert Whitman, 1986. Ages 5–9.

Jason wants his grandmother to come home, but she has Alzheimer's disease and must stay in a nursing home. His first visits to her are filled with disturbing experiences, and Grandma does not recognize Jason. Eventually, Jason understands that Grandma needs his companionship despite her forgetfulness. An adequate introduction to this disease of aging.

General

Bad Luck Tony, Dennis B. Fradin, Ill. by Joanne Scribner, Prentice-Hall, 1978. O.P. Ages 6–9.

Tony's happiness with the beginning of Christmas vacation and the expected arrival of his grandfather is quickly dissipated. His energies instead are spent in a frantic search for a place for a stray dog to have her puppies. His resolution of the dog's problem promises to make a difference in Tony's life.

Carnival and Kopeck and More about Hannah, Mindy W. Skolsky, Harper, 1979. Ages 7–10.

Hannah convinces her grandmother to take her to a carnival and vows to behave. Grandmother refuses to stay when excited Hannah breaks her promise. They have their first argument. Appalled, Hannah decides to suppress her anger. Grandmother helps Hannah understand that arguments naturally occur when people love each other. *Highly recommended*.

Freddy, My Grandfather, Nola Langner, Four Winds Pr., 1979. Ages 5–8.

A young girl describes her Hungarian-born grandfather, Freddy, who lives with her family. Freddy's room smells like cigars and lemons. He makes coats just for her, takes her to special places, and comforts her during storms. Sometimes his presence causes tension, but above all, she loves Freddy.

Grandma without Me, Judith Vigna, Albert Whitman, 1984. Ages 4–8.
After his parents' divorce, a young boy misses his paternal grandmother. This year he cannot spend Thanksgiving with her. Both keenly feel their loss. His grandmother sends him a scrapbook, and the two continue their special relationship by stocking the book with mementos. A simple yet sensitive treatment of a common problem.

Ⓡ *Grandmama's Joy*, Eloise Greenfield, Ill. by Carole Byard, Putnam, 1980. Ages 6–9.
Rhondy cannot understand Grandmama's sadness, and her attempts to cheer Grandmama up fail. Crying, Grandmama reveals that she cannot pay the rent and therefore they must move. Rhondy will miss the house, too, but she reminds Grandmama of something; Grandmama has always said that Rhondy is her joy. Now Rhondy realizes that Grandmama is her joy also. *Highly recommended*.

Magic and the Night River, Eve Bunting, Ill. by Allen Say, Harper, 1978. O.P. Ages 6–9.
Yoshi's grandfather has fished for forty years from a rented boat that Kano, the owner, threatens to rent to a more productive fisherman. However, Grandfather triumphs with the aid of his faithful cormorants. When freed because of a fire, the birds return with an enormous catch. Recommended for the respect shown to a grandfather.

Mandy's Grandmother, Liesel M. Skorpen, Ill. by Martha Alexander, Dial, 1975. O.P. Ages 5–8.
Grandmother's visit does not start out pleasantly. Mandy prefers jeans and frogs to the dresses and dolls her grandmother likes. One morning she finds Grandmother crying, and Mandy's sensitivity dissolves their barriers. Grandmother holds Mandy in her lap, and they discover what they can learn from each other. *Highly recommended*.

My Grandpa Retired Today, Elaine Knox-Wagner, Ill. by Charles Robinson, Albert Whitman, 1982. Ages 5–8.
Margey is the only child attending her grandfather's retirement party. She helps clean his barbershop, then watches him lock the door for the final time. Margey and her grandfather try to cheer each other up on this sad occasion. Because of her empathy, Margey is able to help her grandfather look forward to the next day.

When James Allen Whitaker's Grandfather Came to Stay, Martha W. Hickman, Ill. by Ron Hester, Abingdon, 1985. Ages 7–9.
When his widowed grandfather comes to live with James Allen's fam-

ily, they welcome him and try to make him happy. Grandfather strives to adjust, but things aren't right. Despite pleas from the loving family, Grandfather decides to return to his home. A simplistic account, but it exemplifies the need to respect a grandparent's independence.

Parents Working/Not Working

Both My Parents Work, Katherine Leiner, photographs by Steve Sax, Watts, 1986. Ages 5–10.

Ten children, ages 5–14, each describe what it is like to have both parents working. Families from all walks of life help portray the kinds of jobs parents have, how their working affects the families' schedules, and what the children's lives are like. Black-and-white photographs enhance the text.

Daddy and Ben Together, Miriam B. Stecher, photographs by Alice S. Kandell, Lothrop, 1981. Ages 3½–7.

Ben and Daddy take care of each other when Mommy goes on a business trip. They always had fun before, but back then Mommy was always waiting for them. Things don't go well until Ben remembers his mother's advice "to laugh a lot." Contains black-and-white photographs.

Matthew and His Dad, Arlene Alda, Simon and Schuster, 1983. Ages 4–7.

A black-and-white photo–documentary about six-year-old Matthew's relationship with his dad. When Dad works, Matthew thinks there isn't enough time for being together, but he finds there's even less time for fun when Dad is unemployed. The book barely touches on the effects of job loss, but it excellently depicts a father-son relationship.

My Mom Got a Job Today, Lucia B. Smith, Ill. by C. Christina Johanson, Holt, 1979. O.P. Ages 5–7.

A young girl describes the transitions she and her parents go through when her mom gets a job. Monday through Sunday routines are changed, and Mom no longer takes care of the family chores; now everyone helps. While old activities are missed, new ones bring happy times.

My Mother Lost Her Job Today, Judy Delton, Ill. by Irene Trivas, Albert Whitman, 1980. Ages 4–8.

Mother arrives home and announces to six-year-old Barbara Anne that she has lost her job. In mother's silence, the girl envisions a bleak future devoid of parties and Christmases. When Barbara Anne offers to go to work, her mother reassures her that their lives can be the same, although it may take a while.

Sonya's Mommy Works, Arlene Alda, Messner, 1982. Ages 5–8.

Sonya cares for herself and spends time after school with Sarah, her babysitter, because her mother works full time. Sonya worries that her parents won't come to her play and misses her mother when she is away on business. This excellent nonfiction book shows the family's special weekends and Mommy's return for Sonya's sixth birthday.

®   *The Terrible Thing That Happened at Our House*, Marge Blaine, Ill. by John C. Wallner, Macmillian, 1980. Repr. 1975 ed. Ages 5–8.

From a girl's stereotyped viewpoint, her parents cease being a real mother and father when Mom gets a job. Dad does the cooking, and Mom has the car serviced. Worse yet, her parents are inattentive. After the girl's outburst, the family makes changes that allow them to share more time.

Remarriage and Stepfamilies

The Big Red Barn, Eve Bunting, Ill. by Howard Knotts, Harcourt, 1979. Ages 5–8.

The old red barn shelters a boy in his pain when his mom dies and later when his father remarries. When fire destroys the refuge, the boy is forced to face the changes in his life. The boy's grandpa helps him sort out his ambivalent feelings about the new aluminum barn and about his stepmother.

Daddy's New Baby, Judith Vigna, Albert Whitman, 1982. Ages 4–7.

While visiting her father and his new wife, a young girl's space and time are invaded by her baby half-sister. Frustrated with the baby's crying, the girl entertains the child with puppets. Daddy's positive interpretation of the baby's response helps the girl perceive her sister differently. A simplistic but satisfactory introduction to stepfamilies.

Eliza's Daddy, Ianthe Thomas, Ill. by Moneta Barnett, Harcourt, 1976. O.P. Ages 5–7.

Eliza's parents are divorced, and her father is remarried. One night she dreams that his stepdaughter is beautiful and rides a splendid horse. Eliza is jealous and asks Daddy if she can meet his new family. To her amazement, Eliza finds a common bond with the other child.

Everett Anderson's 1-2-3, Lucille Clifton, Ill. by Ann Grifalconi, Holt, 1977. O.P. Ages 4–7.

When Mr. Tom Perry moves into Everett Anderson's apartment building and starts seeing his mother, Everett thinks about numbers. One is lonely; two is just right; but three, Everett decides, is a crowd. Seeing

Mama's obvious happiness about marrying Mr. Perry makes Everett change his mind: three can be just right.

Like Jake and Me, Mavis Jukes, Ill. by Lloyd Bloom, Knopf, 1984. Ages 6–10.

Alex emulates his stepfather, Jake, who is large, strong, and brave. While Alex's pregnant mother relishes a golden autumn evening out alone, she misses the cautious but hilarious proceedings of Alex saving Jake from the wolf spider. A delightful story of a blended family.

My Mother's Getting Married, Joan Drescher, Dial Pr. Bks., 1986. Ages 4–8.

Katy thinks the idea of her mother getting married "stinks." Things are just right for the two of them without Ben. In defiance, Katy wears jeans under her flowergirl's dress at the wedding, but as mom leaves for her honeymoon, she reassures Katy of her continued love.

Ⓝ *Sarah, Plain and Tall*, Patricia MacLachlan, Harper, 1985. Ages 7–11.

Sarah answers Papa's advertisement for a wife and comes from Maine to visit the homestead. As Sarah's independent spirit flourishes, the children, Anna and Caleb, become increasingly anxious about losing her. Returning from a trip to town, Sarah reassures the children that she loves them more than she misses the sea near where she used to live. An excellent departure from the usual reluctance of accepting a stepparent.

She's Not My Real Mother, Judith Vigna, Albert Whitman, 1980. Ages 4–8.

While visiting his father and his father's new wife, Miles becomes concerned that his acceptance of her would be disloyal to his mother. When Miles' trickery causes him to get lost, the two come to an understanding. Before going home, he forms a friendship with his father's wife. A simple approach to a common dilemma.

Separation

Amifika, Lucille Clifton, Ill. by Thomas DiGrazia, Dutton, 1977. O.P. Ages 3–7.

Amifika's daddy is coming home from the army. Mama says she'll make room in their small apartment by getting rid of things Daddy doesn't remember. Amifika cannot remember Daddy and fears that he himself may also be discarded. Desperate, he tries to hide. Awaking in Daddy's arms, Amifika knows the joy of remembering.

Breakfast with My Father, Ron Roy, Ill. by Troy Howell, Houghton, 1980. Ages 4–7.

David's parents are separated, yet every Saturday morning he and his father go out for breakfast. It is a beloved ritual, but then one Saturday his father does not wake him. David is sad when he gets up, but finds his father there for breakfast with the family.

Dear Daddy, Phillipe Dupasquier, Bradbury Pr., 1985. Ages 4–7.

Sophie writes a letter to her father, who is away working on a cargo ship. Two sets of illustrations show Sophie in her home environment and Daddy working at sea over a time span of four seasons. The final illustrations, without text, depict a joyous and tearful reunion.

First Pink Light, Eloise Greenfield, Ill. by Moneta Barnett, Crowell, 1976. O.P. Ages 4–7.

Daddy is coming home after a month's absence. Tyree wants to hide all night and surprise him, but Mama suggests waiting in the chair and hiding at the first pink light of dawn. A sleeping Tyree misses the joy of surprise but feels the closeness of Daddy carrying him to bed.

I Wish I Had My Father, Norma Simon, Ill. by Arieh Zeldich, Albert Whitman, 1983. Ages 5–8.

Father's Day brings longing and sadness to a young boy whose father left home when the boy was a baby. The love of his mother, grandfather, uncles, and neighbor cannot fill the emptiness he feels. The boy maintains the hope of one day meeting his father. A contrived but useful introduction to separation for children deserted by a parent.

If You Listen, Charlotte Zolotow, Ill. by Marc Simont, Harper, 1980. Ages 4–8.

A girl questions how she can know if her father loves her, since he has been gone a long time. Mother tenderly tells her to listen intently for the love being sent, as one listens for sounds in the distance. The child promises to try, but longs for her father's return.

Jafta's Father, Hugh Lewin, Ill. by Lisa Kopper, Carolrhoda, 1983. Ages 4–7.

Jafta misses his father, who has taken a job in the city, away from home. When a friend says that Jafta's father will never return, Jafta's mother assures him that this is not so. Jafta remembers the joys he and his father shared in previous seasons. Winter is almost over, and soon his father will return to their African home.

Neighborhood Knight, Eleanor Schick, Greenwillow, 1976. O.P. Ages 6–8.

A young boy copes with his father's absence by imagining himself as a knight. His mother and sister are the queen and princess whom he must protect; their city apartment, a castle. His fantasy enables the boy to cope with problems and to experience happiness with his mother and sister.

That Is That, Jeanne W. Peterson, Ill. by Deborah Ray. Harper, 1979. O.P. Ages 5–8.

Emma Rose refuses to say good-bye to her father when he leaves their family. But her "magical spells" do not bring him back. In time, Emma Rose is able to accept her father's absence, and Meko, her brother, echoes her thoughts by exclaiming "that is that." Reflects the conflicts a child experiences when a parent leaves.

Sibling Rivalry

All Because I'm Older, Phyllis R. Naylor, Ill. by Leslie Morrill, Atheneum, 1981. Ages 5–9.

John's younger brother constantly undermines him. When Dad takes the boys and baby Stephanie shopping, John wants things to go well, but the outing is a disaster. Finally, John puts a shopping bag over Stephanie, keeping them all amused and out of trouble. For any child who feels manipulated by younger siblings.

A Baby for Max, Kathryn Lasky and Maxwell B. Knight, photographs by Christopher G. Knight, Scribner, 1984. Ages 4–7.

With the arrival of a new sister, five-year-old Max reacts to changes in the family. Max doesn't want his clothes moved and misses his parents' attention, but he likes helping out with his sister Maribah and being a big brother. A photo-study of the mixed emotions accompanying the arrival of a new sibling.

Big Boss! Little Boss!, Barbara Bottner, Pantheon, 1978. Ages 6–8. An I am reading book.

Two stories about Penny, big boss, and Lizzie, little boss. In the first story, Penny derides Lizzie's carelessness with possessions and finds Lizzie's precious Mickey Mouse ring. In the second, Lizzie grants Penny's birthday wish by pretending that she is the older sister. Penny is sloppy, cries, and is cuddled by Lizzie for an afternoon. An entertaining portrayal of sibling roles.

Bright Fawn and Me, Jay Leech and Zane Spencer, Ill. by Glo Coalson, Crowell, 1979. Ages 5–8.

When two Cheyenne sisters attend a trading fair, everyone tells the big sister that the younger one, Bright Fawn, is wonderful. In return, the older girl either ignores the comment or offers criticism. Her reaction to Bright Fawn changes when another girl harasses them. A story for all sisters.

Chuckie, Nicki Weiss, Greenwillow, 1982. Ages 4–7.

Lucy is a good girl until the arrival of her new baby brother, Chuckie.

First she pretends he doesn't exist; then she calls him names and blames him for her misbehavior. Nothing makes Chuckie disappear, and nothing seems to bother him. When Chuckie's first word is "Lucy," everything changes. Contains delightful illustrations.

The Crack-of-Dawn Walkers, Amy Hest, Ill. by Amy Schwartz, Macmillan, 1984. Ages 5–8.
Sadie and her younger brother, Ben, reach an agreement to alternate turns for the early Sunday morning walk with Grandfather. Today it is Sadie's turn to be alone with Grandfather. As they walk and shop, Sadie and her grandfather discuss Sadie's concerns about sharing Grandfather with Ben. An unusual approach to sibling rivalry.

Don't Touch My Room, Patricia Lakin, Ill. by Patience Brewster, Little, 1985. Ages 4–8.
Aaron doesn't want to share his room with his new sibling. His parents surprise Aaron with a secret refuge in his remodeled room, but things are just as bad as Aaron anticipated until Benji gradually works his way into Aaron's affections. Aaron offers his brother refuge when Benji's naughtiness irritates their parents.

Good-Bye, Arnold!, P.K. Roche, Dial, 1979. Ages 4–7.
Webster hates his big brother, Arnold, for not sharing, being bossy, and acting self-important. His dream that his big brother leaves home comes true when Arnold goes to visit Grandma. The intense joy of being alone gradually dissipates in the quiet, and Webster eagerly welcomes Arnold's return.

Great-Grandfather, the Baby, and Me, Howard Knotts, Atheneum, 1978. O.P. Ages 5–8.
A young boy seeks out the comfort of his great-grandfather while waiting for his parents to bring home his new baby sister. The old man eases the child's unspoken apprehension by telling about his long ago journey on horseback for a glimpse of a baby he didn't even know. *Highly recommended.*

Grouchy Uncle Otto, Alice Bach, Ill. by Steven Kellogg, Harper, 1977. Ages 5–8.
Rich, grouchy Uncle Otto has a broken arm. Oliver Bear is determined to care for him better than his smart twin brother, Ronald, can. Otto tries Oliver's patience, so the twins switch places. Otto isn't fooled by or impressed with Ronald's care. He warns Ronald about his cleverness and shows appreciation for Oliver's humility.

Harriet and Walt, Nancy Carlson, Carolrhoda, 1982; Penguin, 1984. Ages 4–8.
Harriet the dog considers it a nuisance to take her brother, Walt, to play

in the snow and disparages him for spoiling her games. When her friend, George the rabbit, joins in the criticism, she defends Walt. Leaving George, Harriet shows Walt how to do the things he failed at earlier.

Henrietta and the Gong from Hong Kong, Winifred Rosen, Ill. by Kay Chorao, Four Winds Pr., 1981. Ages 5–8.

Henrietta refuses lunch while visiting her grandparents, so she is not served chocolate cake. Reaching for a lick of icing, Henrietta knocks over the cake, and her flight to avoid punishment causes further disaster. Feeling inadequate in comparison to her almost perfect sister, Henrietta learns that she is like her mother as a child. *Highly recommended*.

Henrietta, the Wild Woman of Borneo, Winifred Rosen, Ill. by Kay Chorao, Four Winds Pr., 1975. O.P. Ages 5–8.

Evelyn is pretty and neat, but Henrietta has bushy hair and is sloppy. Frustrated with her sister's unkindness and her parents' nagging, Henrietta decides to go to Borneo. Her attempt to mail herself there is foiled when her family opens the crate she has packed herself in. The family reassures her that they all want their "wild woman." *Highly recommended*.

I Hate My Brother Harry, Crescent Dragonwagon, Ill. by Dick Gackenbach, Harper, 1983. Ages 4–7.

Harry's little sister hates him. He's mean and deceptive, although occasionally kind. After their mother tells her about Harry's amiability during her infancy, she puts him to a test. Harry responds with an unspoken declaration of friendship. She is pleased but knows that Harry will continue to be mean sometimes.

I Think He Likes Me, Elizabeth Winthrop, Ill. by Denise Saldutti, Harper, 1980. Ages 4–7.

Eliza keeps trying to tell her parents that her new baby brother likes her, but they do not listen. Instead, they are concerned when she holds Andrew or brings him inappropriate toys. One day when both parents are busy, Andrew wails and Eliza proves that she can care for him.

I Want a Brother or Sister, Astrid Lindgren, Ill. by Ilon Wikland, Harcourt, 1978. Ages 4–7.

Envious of a friend, Peter requests a brother or sister. Surprisingly, Mama promises he will get one. When baby Lena arrives and demands their parents' attention, Peter doesn't like her. Peter's jealousy and aggression surface in many ways. Finally, Mom's reassurance of love and her appeal for Peter's help with Lena resolves Peter's feelings.

If It Weren't for Benjamin (I'd Always Get to Lick the Icing Spoon), Barbara S. Hazen, Ill. by Laura Hartman, Human Sci. Pr., 1979. Ages 4–8.

A young boy describes his feelings about his older brother, Benjamin.

Benjamin has special privileges, causes trouble, and only occasionally is his younger brother's friend. Sometimes his family seems to favor Benjamin, but each reassures little brother about his value and their love for him. His mother helps him understand the ambivalent relationship between siblings. *Highly recommended.*

Jenny's Baby Brother, Peter Smith, Ill. by Bob Graham, Viking, 1981. Ages 3^{1}/$_{2}$–7.

Jenny doesn't think her baby brother, Pete, is worth much. He gurgles, makes a mess with his food, and can't play with her. Pete finally shows some redeeming qualities when he flips food into Jenny's face and starts to imitate her. His mischievousness and spirit win Jenny as a playmate.

Katie Did!, Kathryn O. Galbraith, Ill. by Ted Ramsey, Atheneum, 1982. Ages 4–7.

Mary Rose thinks she is helping her mother care for her new brother, but her mother thinks differently. When Mary Rose realizes her mother's view, she blames her doll, Katie, for the mess. In a confrontation, her mother lets Mary Rose know that she is loved and then finds the time to play with her.

Katie Did It, Becky B. McDaniel, Ill. by Lois Axeman, Childrens Pr., 1983. Ages 6–7. Rookie reader.

Whenever someting goes wrong, Katie's older brother and sister are quick to blame her for being the culprit. It's finally Katie's turn to say "Katie did it" when their mother is pleasantly surprised with flowers and asks who gave them to her. For any young child who feels frequently and unjustly accused.

Keep Running, Allen!, Clyde R. Bulla, Ill. by Satomi Ichikawa, Crowell, 1978. Ages 4–7.

Allen is constantly hurrying to keep up with his older sister and brothers. Whenever he catches up with them, it is time to rush off. Finally, Allen falls on a hillside and experiences the sheer joy of nature. When his siblings tumble down, ridiculing him, they discover the bliss of his quiet time.

Let's Be Friends Again!, Hans Wilhelm, Crown, 1986. Ages 3–7.

Sometimes being an older brother is great; at others it is not so good. One terrible day, little sister sets her brother's pet turtle free, and big brother is so mad that he thinks he can never forgive her. Humorous illustrations accompany this perceptive story of how big brother overcomes his anger. *Highly recommended.*

Lucky Stiff!, Gen LeRoy, Ill. by J. Winslow Higginbottom, McGraw-Hill, 1981. Ages 5–8.

Anabel thinks that her new brother, Vaughn, is a lucky stiff. Her parents lavish him with love and attention, which she feels is undeserved. While playing house with her friends, Anabel, pretending to be a baby, experiences the total helplessness Vaughn must endure. Her newfound understanding allows her to accept her sibling.

Margaret and Taylor, Kevin Henkes, Greenwillow, 1983. Ages 6–9.

In seven episodes, Margaret tries to take advantage of her younger, guileless brother, Taylor. She prompts Taylor to open mail, tantalizes him with left-over birthday cake, and teases him about his airborne balloon. Taylor triumphs, however, when Mother overlooks the opened mail, Margaret forgets her cake, and the wind captures Margaret's balloon.

Maude and Walter, Zibby Oneal, Ill. by Maxie Chambliss, Lippincott, 1985. Ages 4–7.

Four stories about siblings Walter and Maude. Walter ignores his little sister unless she has something he needs. When Maude benefits from having a cold, he develops similar symptoms. Maude wins again when Walter becomes jealous of her imaginary friend and helps her clean up to gain her friendship. For all younger siblings.

Monnie Hates Lydia, Susan Pearson, Ill. by Diane Paterson, Dial, 1975. Ages 5–8.

Monnie's generous preparations for her sister Lydia's surprise birthday party are not acknowledged, and Lydia is downright nasty to her. Daddy asks Monnie to be a good sport. When Lydia's gibes prove too much, Monnie throws the birthday cake, giving Lydia a chance to prove her own sportsmanship. *Highly recommended.*

Much Bigger Than Martin, Steven Kellogg, Dial, 1976. Ages 4–7.

Henry is tired of catering to his older brother, Martin. He tries to stretch, waters himself, and gorges on apples, but nothing makes him bigger. His parents are reassuring, and Martin even shows some sensitivity toward Henry. Through his own determination, Henry finally devises a way to tower over his brother. Contains humorous illustrations.

My Brother Fine with Me, Lucille Clifton, Ill. by Moneta Barnett, Holt, 1975. O.P. Ages 5–8.

While Mama and Daddy work, Johnny has to watch her younger brother Baggy, who is a pest. Therefore, she is only too happy to help Baggy pack when he decides to run away. Alone, Johnny experiences emptiness and is happy to find that Baggy has returned home. Uses sensitive pencil illustrations.

Ⓡ *My Mama Needs Me*, Mildred P. Walter, Ill. by Pat Cummings, Lothrop, 1983. Ages 4–7.

On the day his new sister comes home, Jason won't play with friends and refuses cookies from a neighbor. Telling everyone that "my Mama needs me," Jason's true concern is that he's not really needed. At last, Mama assures Jason that he is definitely needed, both for his hugs and for his help.

Oink and Pearl, Kay Chorao, Harper, 1981. Ages 6–8. An I can read book.
   Four stories about Oink and Pearl Pig that reflect the love-hate relationship between siblings. In one story, Pearl bemoans having a little brother, but Oink, her brother, comforts her when she's hurt. In another story, Pearl's jealousy over Auntie's favoritism of Oink is diffused when she discovers that Oink doesn't like being gushed over.

Ⓡ *Poinsettia and Her Family*, Felicia Bond, Crowell, 1981. Ages 4–7.
   Poinsettia Pig's house is quite fine, except for her six brothers and sisters and parents. Sensing the overcrowding, her father takes the family to search for a larger home, but selfish Poinsettia manages to be left behind. That evening, distraught by loneliness, she is overjoyed at her family's return.

Princess Pearl, Nicki Weiss, Greenwillow, 1986. Ages 5–7.
   Rosemary taunts and dominates her younger sister, Pearl. When Pearl's friend, Janie Sachs, comes to visit, Rosemary witnesses Pearl's victimization by an outsider. The insight results in Rosemary's putting aside her sibling rivalry and becoming Pearl's ally. Contains humorous illustrations.

Quilts in the Attic, Robbin Fleisher, Ill. by Ati Forberg, Macmillan, 1978. Ages 3–6.
   Rosie wants to be everything her older sister, Natasha, pretends to be as they play with quilts in the attic. Natasha angrily threatens her sister not to be a copycat. By being as quiet as a quilt, Rosie ends the argument and plays happily with Natasha.

Superduper Teddy, Johanna Hurwitz, Ill. by Susan Jeschke, Morrow, 1980. Ages 5–9.
   Six stories, which can be enjoyed separately, about rivalry and camaraderie between Teddy and his older sister, Nora. Unlike Nora, Teddy is shy. Teddy's steps toward overcoming his shyness and achieving independence include attending a party alone, getting a job watching the neighbor's cat, and entertaining his kindergarten class.

Too Big, Holly Keller, Greenwillow, 1983. Ages 3–6.
   Henry the opossum is told that he is "too big" for many things when baby brother Jake arrives. Henry's antics to deal with the newcomer's arrival are all thwarted until he finally learns the meaning of being "too big." However, Mama shows Henry that no one outgrows a hug.

When the New Baby Comes, I'm Moving Out, Martha Alexander, Dial, 1979. Ages 3–7.

Oliver is outraged to find his mother refinishing his old possessions for the expected baby. He proposes taking her to the dump, or else he'll leave. Mother empathetically tells Oliver that she would miss him. As they reconcile, mother and son share their different visions of the joys of being an older brother.

The Witch Who Was Afraid of Witches, Alice Low, Ill. by Karen Gundersheimer, Pantheon, 1978. O.P. Ages 4–7.

Wendy is the youngest of three witch sisters. Her lack of confidence in her witch power is reinforced by her belittlement by the older witches. On Halloween, a little ghost helps Wendy develop her power with an old broomstick. The magic helps Wendy get even with her sisters and win their respect.

Related Titles

General

Family Relationships
I Love You Mouse, John Graham.

The Year of Mr. Nobody, Cynthia King.

Problems at Home
Don't Hurt Me Mama, Muriel Stanek.

Michael, Liesel Skorpen.

Sibling Relationships
Arthur's Pen Pal, Lillian Hoban.

Backyard Basketball Superstar, Monica Klein.

Best Friends for Frances, Russell Hoban.

David and Dog, Shirley Hughes.

The Monster in the Third Dresser Drawer, Janice Smith.

No Boys Allowed, Susan Terris.

The Wild Swans, Hans Christian Andersen.

Grandparents

General

Blackberries in the Dark, Mavis Jukes.

Buffy and Albert, Charlotte Pomerantz.

Chin Chiang and the Dragon's Dance, Ian Wallace.

Grandma's House, Elaine Moore.

Grandpa and Bo, Kevin Henkes.

Grandpa, Me, and Our House in the Tree, Barbara Kirk.

Now One Foot, Now the Other, Tomie de Paola.

When I Was Young in the Mountains, Cynthia Rylant.

Parents Working/Not Working

All Alone after School, Muriel Stanek.

The Bad Dreams of a Good Girl, Susan Shreve.

George the Babysitter, Shirley Hughes.

Home Alone, Eleanor Schick.

Martin by Himself, Gloria Skurzynski.

My Daddy Don't Go to Work, Madeena S. Nolan.

My Mom Travels a Lot, Carolyn F. Bauer.

My Mommy Makes Money, Joyce S. Mitchell.

On My Own: Kids' Self-Care Book, Lynnette Long.

The Sweeneys from 9-D, Ethel and Leonard Kessler.

Tight Times, Barbara S. Hazen.

Separation

Fearless Leroy, Osmond Molarsky.

I Love My Mother, Paul Zindel.

Sibling Rivalry

Friday the 13th, Steven Kroll.

Chapter 7

Fears

Bravery
General
Getting Lost
Monsters
Nighttime Fears
Specific Fears
Storms

The experience of fear is universal, although its focus may change throughout life. Children experience many real fears, including fears that, to adults, seem unfounded. While a two-year-old's developing imagination brings fear of nebulous creatures, the three-year-old is terrorized by individual make-believe monsters. In later years, fears become more specific and definable, such as ghosts, thunder, and sirens. Nightmares and terrors are common for all children under age six; so, too, are fears of bodily harm, animals, death, and separation.

At times, children may find excitement in scaring themselves or others. In such a case, fears may be seen as a challenge to their bravery, especially when they know that a safe retreat awaits them. However, unbidden fears are the most common and create anxiety for children.

Stress caused by fear may be compounded by accompanying feelings of embarrassment, isolation, or helplessness. Young children are often unable to describe their emotions and, at times, to say "I am afraid." By age five, youngsters are more able to discuss their feelings, but they may need help expressing them. It is the responsibility of adult caregivers to be aware of the signs of fear in a child and to provide the necessary intervention.

When adults are not aware of a child's fears, the fears may intensify. The child needs the fear to be acknowledged and taken seriously, and the reassurance to deal with it. Caregivers should be aware of the difference between a child's imagination and adult reasoning. Children should not be ridiculed for their fears; children need acceptance in order to begin dealing with their concerns. Adults can provide realistic explanations, answer objections, and encourage children to express their feelings. One way to facilitate this interaction is through the use of books.

Numerous books that allow children to see others in a situation similar to their own are available on specific fears. Stories can clarify and define the things that frighten children. Honest information shared with true concern can prevent children from developing a distorted perception of the things they fear. Careful selection of books and their use as communication aids can help children gain confidence and master their fears. Caregivers should avoid the use of books that treat fears in a frivolous or light manner. Children take their fears seriously, and books selected for them on this subject should respect that fact.

Every day, many children are faced with fearful situations, both real and imagined, that can cause them emotional stress. The books described in this chapter demonstrate many of these fears and offer some insights into them. There are countless children's books dealing with fears, but only those of the highest quality are mentioned in this chapter.

Bravery

® *The Banza*, Diane Wolkstein, Ill. by Marc Brown, Dial, 1981. Ages 5–8.
   Cabree, a goat, and Teegra, a tiger, become friends when frightened by a thunderstorm. After Teegra is reunited with his family, he gives Cabree a banza for protection. Cabree does not understand how the musical instrument can protect him, until he uses it to ward off tigers. A Haitian folk tale.

Cowardly Clyde, Bill Peet, Houghton, 1979. Ages 5–8.
   Clyde, Sir Galavant's horse, is a coward. Clyde's brave facade fools his master, but even the dogs play upon his weakness. When Galavant goes to fight an ogre, Clyde reveals his timidity but overcomes his fear to save his master. A good allegory on the real meaning of bravery.

The Foolish Giant, Bruce and Katherine Coville, Lippincott, 1978. Ages 5–8.
   Harry is a friendly giant, but his good intentions often cause him trouble. The angry people of the town finally order him to leave, not realizing the protection he affords them. Just as the wicked wizard is about to destroy the townspeople, Harry rushes to their rescue. The giant becomes a hero.

The Legend of Scarface: A Blackfeet Indian Tale, Robert San Souci, Ill. by Daniel San Souci, Doubleday, 1978. O.P. Ages 5–8.
   A beautiful rendition of an Indian legend. Scarface, named for a birthmark on his face, falls in love with Singing Rain. Before they can marry, he must travel to the Sun to ask permission. Once there, his humble request is granted because of his kindness and bravery for once saving Morning Star, whose father is the Sun.

A Matter of Pride, Emily Crofford, Ill. by Jim LaMarche, Carolrhoda, 1981. Ages 7–12.

Meg's family must move to a cotton plantation so that her father can find work. Everyone adjusts except Meg's mother, who is afraid of everything. Meg is ashamed until her mother bravely stands up to mean Mr. Bowers. Meg's perception of courage and of her mother are revised.

Not Just Any Ring, Danita R. Haller, Ill. by Deborah Ray, Knopf, 1982. Ages 6–10.

Jessie Yano longs for a magic ring. Her grandfather takes her to buy the ring but also explains that the real magic is in her heart. On the way home, their truck becomes stuck, and Grandfather is injured. Braving a perilous climb to safety, Jessie learns the meaning of her grandfather's wisdom. Contains beautiful illustrations.

Once Upon a Dinkelsbuhl, Patricia Gauch, Ill. by Tomie de Paola, Putnam, 1977. O.P. Ages 4–8.

In this retelling of a German legend, the lovely town of Dinkelsbuhl is silent. Plundered three times by armies, the residents have lost heart. When another army comes and is going to burn Dinkelsbuhl, only Lore, the gatekeeper's daughter, and the other children have the courage to prevent it.

The Red Lion, Diane Wolkstein, Ill. by Ed Young, Crowell, 1977. Ages 5 + .

Azgid, Prince of Persia, must fight the Red Lion before being crowned king. Three times he runs away rather than fight a lion he fears. Finally, a tame lion teaches Azgid that he must face his fears or run forever. Its fairytale quality makes this a story for all ages. *Highly recommended.*

© *Saint George and the Dragon*, Margaret Hodges, Ill. by Trina S. Hyman, Little, 1984. Ages 5 + .

A wonderful story from Spenser's *Faerie Queene* about young George, the Red Cross knight. In answer to Princess Una's search for a dragonkiller, George seeks the dreadful creature that is destroying the land. Overcoming great difficulties and aided by enchantments, he slays the dragon. A book that will enrapture young and old.

Sometimes It Happens, Elinor Horwitz, Ill. by Susan Jeschke, Harper, 1981. Ages 6–8.

Victor tells everyone that he is going to be a hero when he grows up. After his outlandish daydreams precipitate a fight with his best friend, Victor becomes an authentic hero by saving the red bird's nest. With his mother's help, Victor realizes that being a hero means aiding someone or something.

Ⓡ *Wagon Wheels*, Barbara Brenner, Ill. by Don Bolognese, Harper, 1978. Ages 6–8. An I can read history book.

The three Muldie boys move to Kansas in the 1870's. Their story, told by the eldest brother, who is eleven, chronicles the hardships they endure. The boys face the dangers of the wilderness as they travel 150 miles by themselves to meet their father.

Who's in Rabbit's House?, Verna Aardema, Ill. by Leo and Diane Dillon, Dial, 1977. Ages 5–8.

One evening, Rabbit is afraid to go into her house because someone with a fierce voice is in it. Her animal friends offer unsatisfactory help in removing the "Long One." Finally, Small Frog, whose help Rabbit has scorned, drives out the intruder in a surprise ending. The Dillons' colorful illustrations complement this African tale.

William Tell, Nina Bawden, Ill. by Pascale Allamand, Lothrop, 1981. O.P. Ages 6–9.

The brave hunter, William Tell, refuses to bow to the hat of the cruel bailiff, Gessler. Because of his insolence, William must shoot an apple off his own son's head. The valor of William Tell inspires his countrymen to defend their freedom. A simple retelling of a renowned legend.

General

A Book of Scary Things, Paul Showers, Ill. by Susan Perl, Doubleday, 1977. Ages 5–8.

In picture book format, a young boy explains that lots of things are scary. He tells about his own, his family's, and other people's fears, pointing out that some anxieties are justified as real dangers. The message that everyone is afraid of something is communicated in a nondidactic way. Contains humorous illustrations.

Sometimes I'm Afraid, Jane Watson, Robert Switzer, et al., Ill. by Irene Trivas, Crown, 1986. Ages 3–6.

A child of three describes some of the fears he has experienced and how his parents have helped him overcome them. In addition to describing common fears, the authors' inclusion of anxieties involving anger and illness makes this book unique. Includes an excellent note to parents.

Thornton the Worrier, Marjorie W. Sharmat, Ill. by Kay Chorao, Holiday, 1978. Ages 4–8.

Thornton the rabbit worries about everything. His friends cannot convince him that everything is "okay." Finally, Thornton meets a man who is too busy enjoying life to worry that his house is falling off a mountain. As Thornton pulls the man to safety, he realizes the absurdity of excessive worrying. A humorous account of two extremes.

Will It Be Okay?, Crescent Dragonwagon, Ill. by Ben Shecter, Harper, 1977. Ages 4–8.

A conversation between a mother and daughter about the many fears of childhood. The mother gently reassures her child that there are ways to handle each situation, whether imaginary or real. A wonderful story that can help answer some of the "what if" questions raised by young people. *Highly recommended*.

Getting Lost

The Highest Balloon on the Common, Carol Carrick, Ill. by Donald Carrick, Greenwillow, 1977. Ages 4–8.

Paul is excited about old home day in his village. The events of the day are happy ones until Paul is separated from his parents and fears that he's lost. Before real panic sets in, Paul's father is able to find him by spotting the yellow balloon tied to Paul's wrist.

I'll Bet You Thought I Was Lost, Shirley Parenteau, Ill. by Lorna Tomei, Lothrop, 1981. Ages 5–8.

Sandy loves shopping with his father because sometimes he gets treats. However, this time at the supermarket they become separated. As Sandy tries to find his father, he becomes increasingly desperate. But when he accidentally bumps into his father, Sandy glibly tells him, "I'll bet you thought I was lost."

Joseph on the Subway Trains, Kathleen Benson, Ill. by Emily McCully, Addison-Wesley, 1981. O.P. Ages 5–8.

On a field trip, Joseph gets on the wrong subway train. He has been in subways before and does not see any reason to heed his teacher's warning to stay with the class. One mistake leads to another, but finally Joseph admits he is lost and asks for help.

Lost in the Museum, Miriam Cohen, Ill. by Lillian Hoban, Greenwillow, 1979. Ages 5–7.

At the museum, the teacher warns the children to stay together, but some wander off to see the dinosaur. Frightened by the thought of spending the night with the dinosaur, Jim finds the teacher and reunites the class. His bravery is acknowledged by everyone.

Monsters

Clyde Monster, Robert Crowe, Ill. by Kay Chorao, Dutton, 1976. Ages 4–8.

Young Clyde is a typical monster, except for one thing. He is afraid that people are hiding in his cave to scare him at night. His parents reassure him that long ago, monsters and people made an agreement not to frighten each other. Contains delightful illustrations.

Do Not Open, Brinton Turkle, Dutton, 1981. Ages 5–8.

Exploring the beach the morning after a storm, Miss Moody and her cat, Captain Kidd, find a bottle marked "do not open." She opens it despite the warning, and out comes a terrible monster. Miss Moody spurns his power and through her cleverness causes the monster's destruction.

Harry and the Terrible Whatzit, Dick Gackenbach, Clarion, 1977. Ages 4–8.

After his mother goes to the cellar, Harry worries that the monster will get her. Despite his fear, he gingerly creeps down to the smelly, dark cellar and confronts the two-headed Whatzit. Harry drives out the shrinking monster and is relieved to find his mother in the garden. A delightful story.

I'm Coming to Get You!, Tony Ross, Dial Pr. Bks., 1984. Ages 3–7.

A horrifying monster gobbles up whole planets in outer space. The monster decides on Earth's Tommy Wilson as his next victim. While the monster looms outside, young Tommy, sensing its presence, is afraid. When the monster pounces, it's so small that Tommy doesn't even notice it. A humorous help for children who envision monsters as gigantic.

Jim Meets the Thing, Miriam Cohen, Ill. by Lillian Hoban, Greenwillow, 1981. Ages 5–8.

After the movie "The Thing" appears on television, all the first graders want to play Super Heroes, except Jim. His fear, stemming from the program, makes him feel very inadequate. When Jim removes a praying mantis from his classmate Danny's arm, the other children admit some of their fears, thus giving Jim new confidence.

Monster Tracks?, A. Delaney, Harper, 1981. Ages 3–7.

Harry ventures out into the wonderful snow-covered world. He follows large tracks into the woods, but becomes frightened, believing that a great monster is after him. Falling face down in the snow, Harry bravely looks up to find Sam, his dog, and the source of the tracks.

Patrick's Dinosaurs, Carol Carrick, Ill. by Donald Carrick, Clarion, 1983. Ages 5–8.

Walking through the zoo, Patrick's older brother, Hank, describes the great dinosaurs. While they explore the exhibits, Patrick's imagination runs wild, and he envisions the approach of dinosaurs. Although Patrick usually likes to scare himself, this time he does not feel safe until they are back home and Hank assures him that dinosaurs are extinct.

Nighttime Fears

The Bad Dream, Jim Aylesworth, Ill. by Judith Friedman, Albert Whitman, 1985. Ages 4–8.

A young boy's bad dream disrupts the quiet night. While his mother and father sleep peacefully, he dreams of loneliness and fear. A fall from his bed brings the boy's parents to offer him comfort and security. The soft brown-and-blue tones of the book's illustrations convey the mood of the story.

Boris and the Monsters, Elaine Willoughby, Ill. by Lynn Munsinger, Houghton, 1980. Ages 4–8.

In the daytime, Boris feels safe, but at night he has many excuses to avoid going to bed. He is sure that monsters will appear at night. When his parents cannot convince him otherwise, they buy Boris a dog for protection. Instead of the watchdog Boris envisioned, the dog is a puppy whom Boris must comfort instead.

I Had a Bad Dream: A Book about Nightmares, Linda Hayward, Ill. by Eugenie, Golden Bks., 1985. Ages 4–7.

Jason dreams that his brother is drowning. To rescue him, Jason faces the things his brother fears: darkness, dogs, and a giant. Awakening, Jason goes to his father, and together they find his brother safe. Jason realizes it was only a bad dream. A convincing look at how nightmares can be related to reality.

Kate's Quilt, Kay Chorao, Dutton, 1982. Ages 3–6.

Kate is mad! When Mama's surprise for her is a quilt, not a doll, Kate has a tantrum. But Kate's anger is dissipated when she discovers that her quilt can keep her snug and safe from her nighttime fears.

Monster Night at Grandma's House, Richard Peck, Ill. by Don Freeman, Viking, 1977. O.P. Ages 5–8.

August days at Grandma's are wonderful, but Tobey dreads the nights. As Grandma sleeps downstairs in the old house, he stays awake because of the monster. Conquering his fear one night, Tobey chases the imaginary monster out of the house. Reassured by his own bravery, Tobey knows that the monster won't trouble them again.

The Night We Slept Outside, Anne and Harlow Rockwell, Macmillan, 1983. Ages 6–8. Ready-to-read.

Robert and his older brother get new sleeping bags and beg to sleep outside on their deck. When their mother grants their request, the excitement of having an adventure wears off quickly. The strange outdoor noises scare the brothers, but they feign bravery and do not seek shelter until a thunderstorm drives them indoors.

No Elephants Allowed, Deborah Robison, Houghton, 1981. Ages 4–7.

Every night an elephant comes into Justin's room. At first, his family tries to help him by declaring the impossibility of what Justin imagines. Then each in turn gives him something to ward off elephants. But nothing helps until Justin himself thinks of a means to keep the elephants away.

There's a Crocodile under My Bed!, Ingrid and Dieter Schubert, McGraw-Hill, 1981. O.P. Ages 5–8.

Peggy is afraid at bedtime because a crocodile is under her bed. But James, the crocodile, tells her that he is no ordinary crocodile. They play together, and James reveals his mischievous past. He had been sent to the "Land of Man" to comfort children in their nighttime fears and does so with Peggy.

There's a Monster under My Bed, James Howe, Ill. by David Rose, Atheneum, 1986. Ages 4–7.

Simon imagines menacing monsters under his bed, but he refuses to yell, scornful of behaving like his younger brother Alex. Finally, Simon peeks under his bed only to find Alex hiding from other monsters. Simon offers Alex the safety of sleeping with him and in so doing secretly solves his own need for protection.

Ⓡ ***What's under My Bed?,*** James Stevenson, Greenwillow, 1983. Ages 5–8.

Mary Ann and Louie spend the night at Grandpa's. Unnerved by a bedtime story, they imagine horrible things and run to Grandpa for safety. He tells them a tall tale about his own nighttime fears as a child. They come to understand how everyday things can seem scary at night.

Specific Fears

Alfie Gives a Hand, Shirley Hughes, Lothrop, 1983. Ages 3–6.

Alfie takes his old blanket to his friend Bernard's birthday party when he realizes that the invitation does not include his mother. At the party, the blanket provides security for Alfie, since Bernard is being obnoxious. When Bernard frightens Min, Alfie bravely sets aside the blanket to comfort her.

The Biggest, Meanest, Ugliest Dog in the Whole Wide World, Rebecca Jones, Ill. by Wendy Watson, Macmillan, 1982. Ages 3–7.

Jonathan knows he lives next to the biggest, meanest, ugliest dog in the whole wide world—Pirate. He fears and avoids Pirate. But one day there is no one to protect Jonathan, and he cannot hide from Pirate. Because Jonathan bravely stands up to Pirate, they become friends.

Chin Chiang and the Dragon's Dance, Ian Wallace, Atheneum, 1984. Ages 5–8.

Chin Chiang dreams of dancing the dragon's dance with his grandfather. The day of the celebration arrives, but Chin Chiang becomes fearful of being clumsy and flees. He meets an old woman, and because of her he returns to bring his family honor. Contains colorful, detailed illustrations.

The Climb, Carol Carrick, Ill. by Donald Carrick, Clarion, 1980. Ages 5–8.

Brendan, Nora's cousin, is scared when they climb a mountain. Nora, disgruntled at having to entertain Brendan, is not sympathetic. A truce is reached when Nora realizes the extent of Brendan's fears. Later, Nora becomes frightened when trapped in a cave, and a genuine understanding develops between the two.

Dark and Full of Secrets, Carol Carrick, Ill. by Donald Carrick, Clarion, 1984. Ages 5–8.

Christopher is afraid to swim in the pond because it is dark and full of secrets. His father buys him a snorkel and mask and shows him the mysterious underwater world. Despite a real fright later, Christopher's joy in his underwater discoveries triumphs over his fear.

Holes and Peeks, Ann Jonas, Greenwillow, 1984. Ages 2–5.

A delightful look at the difference between holes and peeks in the bathroom from a preschooler's viewpoint. Holes are scary unless fixed or plugged, but peeks are fun because things can be seen through them. The bathroom's black-and-white tile is the background for the book's expressive, colorful illustrations.

Ira Sleeps Over, Bernard Waber, Houghton, 1972. Ages 4–7.

Ira is sleeping over at his friend Reggie's house for the first time. He's excited until his sister teases him about taking his teddy bear. His parents are supportive, but Ira decides to go to Reggie's alone. After Reggie sneaks his bear into bed, Ira runs home for his. *Highly recommended*.

Joey on His Own, Eleanor Schick, Dial Pr. Bks., 1982. Dial easy-to-read. Ages 6–8.

Joey must go to the grocery store alone for the first time. The usual sights and sounds of the city become magnified and frightening. His success at shopping gives Joey the confidence he needs for a relaxed walk home. A good story for fostering independence.

Poinsettia and the Firefighters, Felicia Bond, Crowell, 1984. Ages 4–8.
   Poinsettia Pig is afraid to sleep in her new bedroom. The noises of the old house keep her awake. Suddenly, she sees a fire on the telephone pole in front of her house. Poinsettia is reassured to learn that firefighters stay awake all night to protect people. Helpful for children who are afraid of fires.

Spiders in the Fruit Cellar, Barbara Joosse, Ill. by Kay Chorao, Knopf, 1983. Ages 3–7.
   Elizabeth is big enough to help her mother by going to the cellar, but she is terrified of the spiders down there. Disaster results when Elizabeth goes to the cellar to get peaches. Reasoning does not dispel her fear, so Elizabeth's mother acknowledges that sometimes fears must be outgrown and simply trades jobs with her.

The Train, Robert Welber, Ill. by Deborah Ray, Pantheon, 1972. O.P. Ages 4–8.
   Someone in Elizabeth's family has always taken her to watch the trains, but now everyone is busy. Elizabeth is told she can go alone, but she is afraid to cross the meadow. After a few days, her passion for trains triumphs over her fear, and Elizabeth braves the walk to greet the train.

What's the Matter, Sylvie, Can't You Ride?, Karen Andersen, Dial, 1981. Ages 5–8.
   No matter how hard she tries, Sylvie can't ride her bike. She is scared, and her feet won't stay on the pedals. Endless, futile attempts and teasing from her friend Virginia make anger replace her fear, and soon Sylvie is speeding along. For any child striving to learn a new skill.

Storms

The Bravest Babysitter, Barbara Greenberg, Ill. by Diane Paterson, Dial, 1977. Ages 5–8.
   Heather is Lisa's favorite babysitter—entertaining and always fun. This night, a storm frightens Heather, and a brave Lisa distracts her from the thunder and lightning. A delightful story about role reversal.

Michael, Liesel Skorpen, Ill. by Joan Sandin, Harper, 1975. O.P. Ages 5–8.
   A thunderstorm frightens Michael at night. Throughout the next day, he and his father disagree on several things, including an orphaned rab-

bit that Michael saves. That night, Michael braves a storm to care for the rabbit. He thus overcomes his fear of thunderstorms and resolves the conflict with his father.

Thunderstorm, Mary Szilagyi, Bradbury Pr., 1985. Ages 3–6.

The rumble of thunder from a distance sends a little girl and her dog scurrying to home and mother. As her mother comforts her during the storm, the girl feels safe and is able to offer her dog security. Expressive illustrations evoke the contrasting moods of this simple tale.

Related Titles

Bravery

We Be Warm Till Springtime Comes, Lillie D. Chaffin.

Getting Lost

Out to Sea, Anne and Harlow Rockwell.

Chapter 8

Friendship

Being a Good Friend
Conflicts in Friendship
Establishing New Friendships
No Friends
Nontraditional Friendships

Throughout a person's life, friends are an infinite source of happiness and consolation. From early childhood on, developing friendships becomes a social goal, an essential experience crucial to one's happiness. As a child's horizons expand beyond the family, acceptance by friends becomes his or her greatest need.

Identification with a peer group of accepting and caring friends influences children's self-concepts in a positive way. Sound relationships enable children to perceive themselves as worthy persons. Successfully making friends promotes happiness and a sense of well-being. Failed attempts at friendship and exclusion by peers can be devastating for anyone, but especially for children.

The importance of peer interaction is demonstrated even in infants, who display pleasure and curiosity in the company of other infants. As babies become toddlers, they engage in parallel play, but they enjoy the satisfaction of being near one another. At this young age, they are capable of caring for their playmates, but the development of friendships is a long process.

The skills needed to acquire and maintain friendships have their roots in early childhood and continue to be refined throughout life. It is when children reach preschool that they develop the crucial base from which future friendships will flourish. Indeed, it is the purpose of preschool to teach children to play with other children and to enjoy their companionship.

However, the exhilaration of making new friends is tempered by the realization that these relationships require compromise. The initially egocentric preschooler comes to understand that there is more than one way to view a situation or issue and that personal needs are frequently affected by the needs of others.

The often painful experience of yielding one's desires to meet the needs of another child can be offset for three- and four-year-olds by the joy found in playing together. Three-year-olds can be particularly selfish but will seek out playmates. They do best playing with one other child but are fickle in their relationships. Four-year-olds have a keener interest in developing more stable social relationships and are more interested in group play. Preferences for playmates develop as four-year-olds learn more about themselves and about who is most like them.

Despite the experiences of the preschool years, by age five, children are still not remarkably social. They do best playing with only a couple of friends at a time, but they are different from younger children in their desire to please others and to have interactions go smoothly. There is an increased sense of reciprocity in relationships.

The transition from the preschool to the elementary school years heightens children's desire for friends. The peer group becomes increasingly more significant as a socializing agent, and there is little else that takes precedence over making friends. As they grow older, children develop a community of peers apart from their families and siblings. They depend on peers to provide support, information, and companionship independent of their families.

The struggle to be accepted by other children of the same developmental level is characterized by the ups and downs of relationships. Even at age six, friendships may be easy to acquire but are usually short-term. Although special friends can be at the center of a six-year-old's universe, they still may find it hard to get along. Emotional, aggressive, and competitive behavior, and the criticism of friends at this age do not support stable relationships.

By age seven, friendships are still impeded by rigid standards. Children's personal judgments show little flexibility that would allow empathy in relationships. These hazards are reduced in eight-year-olds, who are better able to show regard for the interests and ideas of their peers. This age group shows increased sophistication for arriving at mutual understanding, reciprocity, and a sense of equality.

The capabilities needed to make and sustain friendships are developed through social experiences with peers and with the assistance of parents and other adults who interact with children. Invariably, parents are concerned about their child's need and desire for friends, and worry when a child despairingly claims, "I have no friends." Most adults can identify with their child's pain as they remember their own social experiences. By understanding the significance of peer acceptance and companionship, parents and other caregivers can help children in a variety of ways without trying to force relationships.

Adults can facilitate the goal of friendship by staying attuned to the needs, feelings, and behaviors of children. Pro-social instincts can be reinforced and anti-social tendencies diminished. Children may need help to put their feelings into words and to avoid either physical aggression or withdrawal into isolation.

Boys and girls, especially at an early age, respond to the leadership offered by their caregivers. Through role-modeling and such activities as play groups, movies, and story telling, adults can help children learn the characteristics of a good friend. The positive characteristics of empathy, cooperation, and respect can be demonstrated for children through real-life situations and through books.

Reading with children can help them understand themselves as distinct individuals with their own needs, and at the same time it can help them become attuned to the needs of others. Characters in stories act out many situations that can aid children in appreciating another person's point of view and in coordinating those views with their own. This understanding can help children who seek acceptance from their peer group.

There are many books whose actions and messages correspond to a child's personal experiences with friendship. These parallels can stimulate children's interest as children come to recognize the relevance these experiences have to their own lives. Caregivers can provide a varied selection of stories that offer boys and girls a choice. For instance, some children may prefer books whose characters reflect their own self-image or who demonstrate qualities admired by the reader. Children also usually can identify with either human or animal characters, but some may have a preference for one type of story or another. Animal characters are often easier to relate to if children are feeling vulnerable in regard to friendships.

The subtle realism found in fictional stories can help boys and girls understand that others also have problems in relationships. Children thus can realize that they are not alone in their feelings of isolation and desire for peer acceptance, and in experiencing conflicts in friendship. Books acknowledge the concerns of children, ease their pain, and offer a sense of hope and confidence.

Stories on friendship, shared between children and their caregivers, can facilitate discussion on the subject. Children can be helped to express feelings otherwise suppressed or not recognized. Parents are then better able to support children in their struggle with the friendships that are so crucial to their happiness.

The books selected for this chapter were carefully chosen to reflect the significance that peer acceptance has for children. Titles that are didactic or demeaning to the subject have been avoided. All the stories in the "Nontraditional Friendships" section are exceptional, and all are highly recommended.

Being a Good Friend

Amy for Short, Laura J. Numeroff, Macmillan, 1976. O.P. Ages 6–8. Ready-to-read.

Best friends Amy and Mark are the tallest children in their class. Returning from camp taller than Mark, Amy fears that she has lost his friendship. Her fears seem to come true when Mark says he can't come to her birthday party. With a special gift and a message, Mark proves his friendship.

The Friend, John Burningham, Crowell, 1976. O.P. Ages 2–6.

The narrator describes his friend Arthur, with whom he plays all the time. Despite their disagreements and their having other friends, Arthur is the boy's best friend. A simple introduction to the concept of special relationships.

Friends, Helme Heine, Atheneum, 1983. Ages 3–7.

Charlie Rooster, Johnny Mouse, and fat Percy Pig are friends. Together they wake the other animals, ride their bike, and sail on the pond. They agree that good friends should stick together, make group decisions, and be fair. However, disaster results when they spend the night with each other and humorously limits their togetherness.

Friends, Satomi Ichikawa, Parents Mag. Pr., 1977. O.P. Ages 3–8.

The necessity and value of friendships are extolled in a simple text and depicted in captivating illustrations. Friends share in the ludicrous and mischievous acts of childhood, show understanding for each other, and delight in the sheer joy of discovery. A tender portrayal of the significance of young friendships.

George and Martha Tons of Fun, James Marshall, Houghton, 1980. Ages 4–8.

Five stories about best friends George and Martha, hippopotamuses. One story deals with a misunderstanding and another with their ability to make each other laugh. In a third tale, Martha takes desperate measures to save George from his sweet tooth. Their hilarious mimicry of human foibles makes these characters a favorite with all ages.

The Great Big Elephant and the Very Small Elephant, Barbara Seuling, Crown, 1977. O.P. Ages 4–8.

While aiding a sick cousin and helping Very Small Elephant entertain a great aunt, Great Big Elephant appears to be the stronger of the two friends. However, in the last story, Very Small Elephant needs to comfort Great Big Elephant, who is terrible at playing games but wonderful at being a friend.

Octavia Told Me a Secret, Marjorie W. Sharmat, Ill. by Roseanne Litzinger, Four Winds Pr., 1979. O.P. Ages 5–8.
Octavia tells a secret to her friend and makes her promise not to tell anyone. Her friend, the narrator, thinks it's such a splendid secret that she visualizes telling or even swapping it. In the end, Octavia's secret is safe because it's her friend's secret also.

Porcupine's Christmas Blues, Jane B. Zalben, Putnam, 1982. Ages 5–8.
Porcupine is melancholy, and his sad singing wakes up Bernard and Phoebe Beaver. Bernard comes to comfort his friend and gently reminds him of his blessings. Porcupine's spirit is renewed by the understanding acceptance he finds in Bernard's friendship, and he goes out to welcome the Christmas morning.

Rosie and Michael, Judith Viorst, Ill. by Lorna Tomei, Atheneum, 1975. Ages 4–9.
Despite Michael's drooping shoulders and Rosie's freckles, they like each other. When Michael sprays whipped cream in Rosie's sneakers and Rosie lets the air out of Michael's basketball, they still remain friends. They call each other when they are hurt, when their pets die, and when their bikes are stolen. A humorous view of a loyal friendship. *Highly recommended*.

Sunny-Side Up, Patricia R. Giff, Ill. by Blanche Sims, Dell, 1986. Ages 6–9.
The inconvenience of summer school is forgotten when Beast learns that his best friend Matthew is moving. The boys scheme to prevent their separation, but they reject the plan when another friend reminds them of Matthew's need for his family. In a tearful parting, the boys promise to remember their good times together.

Ton and Pon: Big and Little, Kazuo Iwamura, Bradbury Pr., 1984. Ages 3–6.
Big Ton and Little Pon are dogs who are pleased with their own size. Each exclaims his advantage in being big or little. As best friends, they can accept their differences along with their individual merits.

Conflicts in Friendship

Battle Day at Camp Delmont, Nicki Weiss, Greenwillow, 1985. Ages 5–8.
Best friends Maude and Sally go to camp. They are inseparable until Battle Day. When chosen for different teams, Maude and Sally help each other. Their teammates point out the unfairness of the girls' divided loy-

alties. A tennis match resolves ambivalent feelings when Maude and Sally work hard for their teams yet still remain friends.

Ⓡ *Best Friends*, Steven Kellogg, Dial Pr. Bks., 1986. Ages 5–8.
Louise and Kathy share the joys and fantasies of best friends. When Louise goes camping, Kathy is lonely and then angry. She plans to fill the void with one of her neighbor's expected puppies. A twist of fate gives Louise the only puppy, but her offer to share ownership rekindles the friendship.

Best Friends for Frances, Russell Hoban, Ill. by Lillian Hoban, Harper, 1969. Ages 4–8.
Albert rejects Frances' friendship because she can't catch frogs and because baseball is labeled a "no-girls game." Therefore, Frances recruits her previously scorned sister, Gloria, to catch frogs and to play ball with her. When she and Albert make up, Frances quells Gloria's fears of rejection by proving that her friendship is lasting. A classic book on friendship.

Clancy's Coat, Eve Bunting, Ill. by Lorinda B. Cauley, Warne, 1984. Ages 5–8.
Tippitt and Clancy have quarreled because Tippitt's cow ruined Clancy's garden. When Clancy brings tailor Tippitt his old coat to repair, the two seem to ignore their former friendship. As weeks pass, the coat goes unfixed for various reasons, but the friendship is gradually mended through the small courtesies they extend to one another.

Come On, Patsy, Zilpha K. Snyder, Ill. by Margot Zemach, Atheneum, 1982. Ages 4–7.
Patsy reluctantly follows her friend to the park. As Patsy struggles to keep up, she hurts her knee, and a dog rips her dress. Things worsen at the park as the friend continues to be selfish and insensitive. Later, the oblivious girl can't understand why she is rejected by Patsy. Illustrations vividly capture Patsy's predicaments and resolution.

A Country Tale, Diane Stanley, Four Winds Pr., 1985. Ages 5–8.
Country cats Cleo and Lucy are close friends until the beguiled Cleo begins to imitate elegant Mrs. Snickers. When Cleo is snubbed on a visit to Mrs. Snickers and robbed on her return, she goes to Lucy. Under her friend's ministrations, Cleo regains her integrity. Tongue-in-cheek humor with a message.

Crystal Is My Friend, Shirley Gordon, Ill. by Edward Frascino, Harper, 1978. O.P. Ages 5–8.
Enjoined by her mother, Susan lets her friend and houseguest, Crystal, have her choice of everything. Crystal chooses Susan's bed, wants to

watch "the News," and makes other selections that displease Susan. When Susan finally gets mad, Crystal agrees that Susan's anger is justified. Together they decide to call "dibs" and remain friends.

Freckles and Willie, Margery Cuyler, Ill. by Marsha Winborn, Holt, 1986. Ages 5–8.

Willie and his dog Freckles are best friends until Jane, the new neighbor, arrives. She hates dogs and criticizes Freckles while monopolizing Willie's time. Freckles feels abandoned until arrogant Jane refuses Willie's valentine. Returning home, Willie makes amends to his reluctant dog and learns the importance of a devoted friendship.

Happy Birthday, Ronald Morgan, Patricia R. Giff, Ill. by Susanna Natti, Viking, 1986. Ages 5–8.

Ronald Morgan is desolate because he will not have a classroom party due to his summer birthday. Then he loses Michael's friendship through unintentional insults. At a teacher's suggestion, Ronald does something nice for Michael. Ronald is overjoyed by the surprise birthday party that's thrown for him on the last day of school and regains Michael's friendship.

The Hiding House, Judith Vigna, Albert Whitman, 1979. Ages 4–7.

Best friends Marybeth and Barbara have an exclusive Hiding House. Their friendship seems doomed when Barbara invites a new neighbor to visit. Outraged, Marybeth locks them out until she overhears Barbara express bewilderment about the offense she has committed against her "best friend." Reassured, Marybeth welcomes both girls as friends.

Hound and Bear, Dick Gackenbach, Clarion, 1976. Ages 4–7.

Three stories about sensible Bear and silly Hound. Twice, Hound plays tricks on Bear, only to lose out on his friend's intended generosity. In the final story, Hound gives wary Bear a real gift and saves their friendship by promising to stop his pranks.

I'm Not Oscar's Friend Anymore, Marjorie W. Sharmat, Ill. by Tony De-Luna, Dutton, 1975. O.P. Ages 4–8.

Oscar and his friend, the narrator, have an argument. For several days, the boy visualizes Oscar moping around the house and not enjoying his favorite television programs. Experiencing the same dilemma, the narrator decides to give Oscar one last chance. The friends are reunited when that narrator learns that Oscar has forgotten the disagreement.

Katharine's Doll, Elizabeth Winthrop, Ill. by Marylin Hafner, Dutton, 1983. Ages 5–8.

Katharine and Molly's friendship is strained when Katharine receives a wonderful doll named Charlotte. When Katharine becomes possessive of the doll, Molly seems to prefer Charlotte to her friend. The girls quarrel. Lonely and bored, Katharine and Molly realize that the doll is no substitute for a real friend, and they reconcile.

The Kid next Door and Other Headaches: Stories about Adam Joshua, Janice L. Smith, Ill. by Dick Gackenbach, Harper, 1984. Ages 6–9.

Five stories about Adam Joshua and his best friend, Nelson, who don't always understand each other, but like each other anyway. Adam Joshua is sloppy, while Nelson is neat. Their opinions about pets and superheroes also differ. They do battle against Nelson's tyrannical cousin and survive a sleepover with their friendship intact. *Highly recommended*.

Losing Your Best Friend, Corinne Bergstrom, Ill. by Patricia Rosamilla, Human Sci. Pr., 1980. Ages 5–8.

A girl describes losing her best friend, Robin, comparing the pain to going somewhere alone for the first time. Trying to win Robin back from their new neighbor, the narrator makes new friends. Best of all, with them she can share something Robin never appreciated: the joy of pretending. A sensitive treatment of a painful problem.

Marinka, Katinka, and Me (Susie), Winifred Madison, Ill. by Miller Pope, Bradbury Pr., 1975. O.P. Ages 7–10.

Before Susie meets Marinka and Katinka on the first day of school, she doesn't have any friends. They become an inseparable threesome. When Marinka and Katinka quarrel, Susie is first paired with one, then the other. Their special relationship seems lost. Finally, the three talk, forget the argument, and regain their treasured friendship. *Highly recommended*.

Meet M and M, Pat Ross, Ill. by Marylin Hafner, Pantheon, 1980. Ages 7–8. An I am reading book.

Inseparable friends Mandy and Mimi live in the same apartment building, share possessions, and cultivate their physical similarities. After an argument, they don't make up as usual. For three days they fume and fret. On a rainy day, via messages sent by rope and pail, the girls finally are able to restore their friendship.

The New Friend, Charlotte Zolotow, Ill. by Emily A. McCully, Crowell, 1968, 1981. Ages 4–8.

A girl describes her friend and their wonderful times together. One day the narrator finds her friend enjoying their treasured activities with another child. Devastated, the girl cries herself to sleep. Dreams of finding a new friend cause her to reflect on the chance of remembering her old friend without pain. *Highly recommended*.

Not at Home?, Bernice Myers, Lothrop, 1981. O.P. Ages 6–8.

Sally is supposed to spend the weekend at her friend Lorraine's house, but on arriving she is told that Lorraine isn't home. Hurt and angry, Sally rushes home and locks herself in her room, missing a phone call from Lorraine. The girls ignore each other until a chance confrontation resolves the misunderstanding.

Patrick and Ted, Geoffrey Hayes, Scholastic, 1984. O.P. Ages 3–5.

Patrick and Ted, little bears, are inseparable best friends. Their identities blend until Ted leaves for the summer. Patrick is lonely, but he learns to enjoy himself. When Ted returns, the two bears squabble, then make up. Both realize that they don't have to do everything together yet can still be best friends.

Starring First Grade, Miriam Cohen, Ill. by Lillian Hoban, Greenwillow, 1985. Ages 5–8.

Jim's unhappiness with his part in the first-grade play makes him bossy and disruptive during rehearsals. This behavior alienates his friend Paul, who does not speak to him for a week. When Paul gets stage fright during the play, Jim proves his friendship by coming to Paul's rescue.

Three Wishes, Lucille Clifton, Ill. by Stephanie Douglas, Viking, 1974. O.P. Ages 4–8.

While walking with her best friend Victorius, Zenobia finds a lucky penny that she believes can bring three wishes. Wasting the first two wishes, Zenobia finds herself alone after an argument with Victorius. With her Mama's advice, Zenobia uses the last wish to ask for the best thing in the world: a good friend. *Highly recommended*.

Unfriendly Book, Charlotte Zolotow, Ill. by William Pene DuBois, Harper, 1975. Ages 4–8.

In this dialogue between Judy and Bertha about their playmates, Judy says that one friend makes her laugh, and another runs fast. According to Bertha, one's a show-off, and another's teeth stick out. Bertha finally accuses Judy of liking everyone. After listening to Bertha's diatribe, Judy replies that actually she does not like Bertha.

Establishing New Friendships

Addie Meets Max, Joan Robins, Ill. by Sue Truesdell, Harper, 1985. Ages 5–7. An Early I can read book.

Max moves in nextdoor to Addie. First his barking dog scares her. After their next encounter when their bikes crash, Addie decides that she wants Max to move away. They finally meet over a lunch arranged by her mother and become friends while discussing their injuries. Humorous illustrations show that Addie's perceptions are different from reality.

Bizzy Bones and Moosemouse, Jacqueline B. Martin, Ill. by Stella Ormal, Lothrop, 1986. Ages 4–7.

While Uncle Ezra travels, Bizzy Bones must stay with Moosemouse. He doesn't like Moosemouse, who is loud and messy. After becoming sick, Bizzy is tenderly cared for by Moosemouse, and his initial prejudice turns to friendship. Their mutual understanding is strengthened as they work together and go to meet Bizzy's returning uncle.

The Candy Corn Contest, Patricia R. Giff, Ill. by Blanche Sims, Dell, 1984. Ages 6–9.

Richard is beginning to hate his friend, smelly Matthew. Richard's anticipated sleepover is being spoiled because no one wants to sleep near Matthew, who wets the bed. After Richard stealthily eats from the candy corn jar, the object of a classroom contest, Matthew helps him out. Richard confesses his misdemeanor and, in return, helps Matthew with his problem.

Crystal Is the New Girl, Shirley Gordon, Ill. by Edward Frascino, Harper, 1976. O.P. Ages 5–8.

Susan does not want to be friends with the new girl, but Crystal won't give up. Almost immediately, zany Crystal is getting Susan into trouble with the teacher. Susan's reticence soon gives way, and the girls become friends. Susan even regrets the summer break because Crystal does not live nearby.

Fast Friends, James Stevenson, Greenwillow, 1979. Ages 6–8. Read-alone book.

Two stories about developing friendships. In one story, Murray the turtle and Fred the snail find that their slow pace is the basis for friendship and for a hilarious adventure. In the second story, Thomas the mouse and Clem the turtle learn about the need for reciprocation in friendship.

Leo, Zach, and Emmie, Amy Ehrlich, Ill. by Steven Kellogg, Dial, 1981. Ages 6–8.

Four stories about Leo and Zach, who are friends, and Emmie, the new girl at school. Emmie's ability to wiggle her ears makes Zach hostile but results in friendship. Later, Zach feels jealous when Leo and Emmie work on a school project together. They soothe him by showing him that they care.

Lizzie and Harold, Elizabeth Winthrop, Ill. by Martha Weston, Lothrop, 1986. Ages 5–8.

Lizzie yearns for a best friend. Despite her mother's advice that special friendships "just happen," she schemes to find a girlfriend. Lizzie scorns

Harold's attempts at friendship until she senses a potential threat to their relationship. Delightful illustrations capture the humor of the story.

Lonely Lulu Cat, Joseph Slate, Ill. by Bruce Degen, Harper, 1985. Ages 4–6.

Lulu Cat is lonely in her new surroundings. In the quiet night, seeking the assistance of Star, Moon, and Owl to see her old friends, Lulu Cat is unaware of the developing new relationships around her. Owl helps her understand how to maintain contact with her old friends while enjoying the blessings of new friendships.

Maude and Sally, Nicki Weiss, Greenwillow, 1983. Ages 4–8.

Maude and Sally are best friends and do everything together. But when Sally goes to summer camp, Maude spends most of the time missing her. Finally, at her mother's suggestion, Maude invites Emmylou over to play. At first, things don't go well, but gradually Maude sees that differences can be good, too.

The School Mouse, Dorothy J. Harris, Ill. by Chris Conover, Warne, 1977. O.P. Ages 5–8.

Jonathan doesn't like first grade, because teacher is sometime cross and he has no friends. Each night he worries, until his old friend, a mouse, reappears. Mouse loves long rides in Jonathan's toy jeep, so Jonathan takes him to school. While his teacher allows Mouse to drive around the halls, Jonathan makes friends.

Timothy Goes to School, Rosemay Wells, Dial, 1981. Ages 4–6.

The teacher is sure that Timothy and Claude, young raccoons, will be good friends, but instead they become rivals. Timothy thinks the arrogant Claude is smart and has all the friends. When Violet, another classmate, shares similar sentiments about her own adversary, she and Timothy discover a common bond and a new friendship.

Where Is My Friend?, Marcus Pfister, North-South Bks., 1986. Ages 18 mos.–3.

A porcupine encounters several objects bearing some resemblance to himself and questions whether they are his friends. His quest culminates in finding someone to answer his needs. A board book for young children on friendship.

Will I Have a Friend?, Miriam Cohen, Ill. by Lillian Hoban, Macmillan 1967. Ages 4–7.

As his father takes him to school for the first time, Jim expresses a desire for a friend. Throughout the day, Jim observes the other children with yearning and anticipation. The boisterous ones are noticeable, but Paul, quiet like himself, becomes Jim's friend. *Highly recommended*.

No Friends

The Lonely Prince, Max Bolliger, Ill. by Jurg Obrist, Atheneum, 1982. Ages 4–8.

Young Prince William doesn't laugh or cry; he just looks sad. His parents anguish over the Prince and buy him anything he thinks will bring happiness. When William pleads with the gardener's boy for his rabbit, the child refuses but offers something that finally makes the prince smile: the gift of friendship.

Moon, Stars, Frogs, and Friends, Patricia MacLachlan, Ill. by Tomie de Paola, Pantheon, 1980. O.P. Ages 4–8.

Randall is a lonely frog until another frog appears. To his dismay, Randall learns that his new friend is Rupert, a bewitched prince. Rupert's unhappiness prompts the benevolent Randall to risk losing his only friend by helping Rupert return to his princely form. In return, Randall is rewarded with his own princess.

No Friends, James Stevenson, Greenwillow, 1986. Ages 5–8.

Mary Anne and Louie hate their new neighborhood because they have no friends. Grandpa tells them a tall tale about his own childhood move. By the end of his story about loneliness, bullies, and new friends, three prospective friends are calling for Mary Anne and Louie. Contains zany illustrations.

The 329th Friend, Marjorie W. Sharmat, Ill. by Cyndy Szekeres, Four Winds Pr., 1979. Ages 4–8.

Emery Raccoon is tired of being alone. To rectify this problem, he invites 328 creatures to lunch. The guests arrive, but they pay no attention to Emery. Distraught, he goes to eat alone. In his solitude, Emery learns something amazing: he enjoys his own company. The self-discovery gives Emery a special friend.

Nontraditional Friendships

The Gift, Helen Coutant, Ill. by Vo-Dinh Mai, Knopf, 1983. Ages 7–11.

Elderly Nana Marie shares her joy in life and nature with fifth-grader Anna. When Nana Marie suddenly becomes blind, Anna spends her day searching the woods for the perfect gift. Until now the recipient, Anna proves her friendship by bringing Nana Marie a "look at the world." *Highly recommended*.

Hi, Mrs. Mallory!, Ianthe Thomas, Ill. by Ann Toulmin-Rothe, Harper, 1979. O.P. Ages 6–10.

A sensitive exploration of friendship between a black child and an elderly, impoverished white woman. During their visits, Mrs. Mallory teaches Li'l Bits the alphabet backwards and tells wonderful stories. Li'l Bits fetches wood and makes out Mrs. Mallory's checks. When Mrs. Mallory dies, Li'l Bits inherits a legacy of memories and a coddled dog. *Highly recommended*.

Miss Maggie, Cynthia Rylant, Ill. by Thomas DiGrazia, Dutton, 1983. Ages 5–8.
Young Nat is fascinated yet revolted by elderly Miss Maggie, who lives nearby. Believing rumors that she keeps a snake, Nat won't enter her house when he delivers food. Investigating the absence of chimney smoke one winter day, Nat discovers Miss Maggie mourning her pet bird, and their special friendship begins. *Highly recommended*.

My War with Mrs. Galloway, Doris Orgel, Ill. by Carol Newsom, Viking/ Penguin, 1985. Ages 7–10.
Eight-year-old Rebecca declares war on her new babysitter, Mrs. Galloway. Whiskers, Rebecca's pregnant cat, is apparently disliked and banished from favorite haunts. Other confrontations result in both Rebecca and Mrs. Galloway being angry. Their worst battle, concerning the birth of Whiskers' kittens, ends in newfound understanding and friendship. *Highly recommended*

A Special Trade, Sally Wittman, Ill. by Karen Gundersheimer, Harper, 1978. Ages 4–8.
Old Bartholomew and his young neighbor, Nelly, are great friends. He tenderly protects her as they walk together and discover new joys. In time, Bartholomew becomes ill, and Nelly sensitively restores her friend's spirits. Their relationship flourishes again as Nelly lovingly returns the care Bartholomew has previously bestowed on her. *Highly recommended*.

Tramp, Malcolm Carrick, Harper, 1977. O.P. Ages 7–10.
In his secret refuge, a shy young boy is safe from other children's mocking until the refuge is invaded by a tramp. First hostile, then welcoming, the boy is desolate to find the tramp gone one day. Examining the quality of that friendship, he makes the first tentative steps in befriending another child. *Highly recommended*.

Related Titles

Being a Good Friend

Badger's Parting Gifts, Susan Varley.

We Are Best Friends, Aliki.

Conflicts in Friendship

Happy Birthday, Crystal, Shirley Gordon.

The Hating Book, Charlotte Zolotow.

I'll Tell on You, Joan Lexau.

Jealousy, Eva Ericksson.

My Best Friend Moved Away, Joy Zelon.

My Naughty Little Sister and Bad Harry's Rabbit, Dorothy Edwards.

Rollo and Juliet, Marjorie W. Sharmat.

Tough Eddie, Elizabeth Winthrop.

The True Francine, Marc Brown.

Two Is Company, Judy Delton.

Establishing New Friendships

All the Cats in the World, Sonia Levitin.

The Beast in Ms. Rooney's Room, Patricia R. Giff.

Everett Anderson's Friend, Lucille Clifton.

Fiona's Bee, Beverly Keller.

Horrible Hannah, Barbara Bottner.

My Friend William Moved Away, Martha W. Hickman.

New Neighbors for Nora, Johanna Hurwitz.

No Friends

Hug Me, Patti Stren.

Nontraditional Friendships

Somebody Else's Child, Roberta Silman.

The Wonderful Mrs. Trumbly, Sally Wittman.

Chapter 9

Hospitalization, Illness, and Health Care

Acute Illness
Chronic Illness
Dentist
Doctor
Emergencies and Accidents
Hospitalization

Sooner or later, every child confronts the challenge of illness and health care issues through routine yet personally trying experiences such as tonsillitis, a trip to the emergency room, or a visit to the dentist. The illness of family members or friends also can profoundly affect a child. The psychological and emotional impact these events bring will be largely determined by the intervention of the caregivers. Adults can influence the child's reaction through acknowledging the significance of these happenings and by providing information, preparation, and support.

Children need to make sense of these difficult events in their lives. Often children are unable to distinguish between reality and fantasy. That is why the sound information and realistic expectations provided by some books can give them a reservoir of strength. Children may worry about what will happen when they or people they care about become ill. Especially at an age when learning to control themselves and their environment is so crucial, a threat to children's well-being can be devastating.

Illness and health care can become an intrusion into a child's life when the child has no sense of control over these events, especially when the child's own health is involved. There are many instances when children, subjected to medical procedures and treatment, view these procedures as punitive. Children may wonder what they have done to deserve such punishment.

A simple visit to the doctor, for instance, may entail a routine immunization, or seeing the dentist may necessitate a Novocaine injection; both are perceived by children as painful. A hospital stay may be even more traumatic because of the care involved, the separation experience, and the child's fear of the unknown. If surgery is required, the psychic trauma may be heightened because the child is afraid that the body part being treated is too important to relinquish.

Whether a child is facing major surgery or a throat culture, it is frightening for him or her to face it unprepared. One way adults can explain such things and reassure children is through books. Books can help children understand the health care experience and cope with the associated anxieties. The greatest benefit can be derived when the books are presented at an appropriate time. For example, a child's first trip to the dentist or doctor can be prefaced by a story about routine health care. Prior to a child's hospitalization, a relevant book can help allay his or her fears of the unknown. Books can open channels of communication between a child and a caregiver. Children may then want to discuss their own reactions to illness and pain, and their perceptions and fears of it. The acknowledgement and expression of feelings during such a crisis can lead to mastery of the experience.

The books included in this chapter are some of the best available to help children overcome the anxieties involved with health care and illness. However, there is still a lack of good children's literature in the areas of chronic illness and mental health.

Acute Illness

Betsy and the Chicken Pox, Gunilla Wolde, Random, 1976. O.P. Ages 3–6.

Betsy's brother is sick, and a doctor reveals that the illness is chicken pox. Feeling ignored, Betsy paints spots on herself, but her demand for attention causes family tempers to flare. Eventually, everyone is mollified, and after caring for baby, Betsy has real spots of her own. The story contains a house visit by the doctor, which is unrealistic today.

I Wish I Was Sick, Too!, Franz Brandenberg, Ill. by Aliki, Puffin, 1978. Ages 3–8.

When her brother, Edward, becomes sick, Elizabeth must still do her chores and go to school. Elizabeth, envious of Edward's special treatment, wishes she were sick, too. A few days later, her wish comes true. After her recovery, Elizabeth and Edward agree that the best part of being sick is getting well.

No Measles, No Mumps for Me, Paul Showers, Ill. by Harriett Barton, Crowell, 1980. Ages 5–8.

Childhood illnesses controlled through immunizations are explained by the young narrator. Information is given regarding specific diseases, how the body fights infection, and the role immunizations play. Although the nonfiction text is generally correct, it should be noted that the explanation of the whooping cough immunization is not accurate.

Phoebe Dexter Has Harriet Peterson's Sniffles, Laura Numeroff, Greenwillow, 1977. O.P. Ages 4–6.

A cold caught from Harriet Peterson causes Phoebe to stay home from kindergarten. At first, she feels forlorn about missing the happenings at school. Eventually, she spends the day creatively in the care of her mother, grandmother, and father.

Sick in Bed, Anne and Harlow Rockwell, Macmillan, 1982. Ages 3–6.

A young boy comes home from school cranky and develops a sore throat. He describes his parents' care, visits to the doctor, and how he spends his days while sick. A good, straightforward approach to the experience of being sick for preschool children, although sponging with alcohol is not safe!

Spots Are Special!, Kathryn O. Galbraith, Ill. by Diane Dawson, Atheneum, 1976. O.P. Ages 4–8.

When Eric teases his sister Sandy about her chicken pox, her ingenuity shows him that spots are special. Sandy's creative play leaves Eric feeling excluded from the "adventure." For any child feeling isolated or embarrassed by chicken pox.

Ⓡ *Teddy Bears Cure a Cold*, Susanna Gretz and Alison Sage, Four Winds Pr., 1984. Ages 3–7.

William the teddy bear is sick, but his friends don't believe him. When he proves it, they lovingly care for him. As William recuperates, he enjoys all the attention. Demanding continued concern after he recovers causes the other teddy bears to rebel. For any malingerer.

Chronic Illness

Anna Joins In, Katrin Arnold, Ill. by Renate Seelig, Abingdon, 1983. Ages 5–8.

Anna is a kindergartner with cystic fibrosis. The ways she sometimes rebels against the disease or occasionally uses it to manipulate others are interwoven into the story of family and school life. The traumas of trying to be a normal child despite the chronic disease are reflected.

Cancer: The Whispered Word, Judy Swenson and Roxane Kunz, Ill. by Jeanette Swofford, Dillon, 1986. Ages 5–10.

Bill's life is disrupted when his mother gets cancer. He explains what he learns about the disease and the changes it causes personally. From the initial diagnosis until her remission, Bill shares his feelings of anger, rebellion, and finally acceptance. Although a milestone on the subject, the book's approach may seem condescending.

Feeling Down: The Way Back Up, Roxane B. Kunz and Judy H. Swenson, Ill. by Mary McKee, Dillon, 1986. Ages 7–12.

Kirk is shocked to learn that his sister Stephanie has attempted suicide. With the help of a therapist, the family learns to communicate and eventually how to cope with their personal and common pressures. An adult resource guide is included. A simplistic approach, but the book is unique in addressing the subject of suicide for this age level.

Grandpa Doesn't Know It's Me, Donna Guthrie, Ill. by Katy Arnsteen, Human Sci. Pr., 1986. Ages 5–8.

When Grandpa's forgetfulness becomes dangerous, he moves in with Lizzie's family. They patiently strive to keep him active and safe. Lizzie describes her fears of Alzheimer's disease, the unpleasantness of being accused of theft by Grandpa, and the anguish of not being recognized. A compassionate portrayal, that is helpful in understanding Alzheimer's disease.

Grandpa, Me and Our House in the Tree, Barbara Kirk, Macmillan, 1978. O.P. Ages 5–8.

Nico is excited because Grandpa is coming to visit, but this time is different. Grandpa is very sick and cannot play ball or climb to the tree house they built together. Nico is lonely and sad until Grandpa rigs up an ingenious phone in order to continue their special relationship.

Harry's Dog, Barbara Porte, Ill. by Yossi Abolafia, Greenwillow, 1984. Ages 6–8. Greenwillow Read-alone.

Harry has acquired a dog, despite his father's allergy. His attempts to hide "Girl" prove futile, and it looks like Harry must give up his pet. But his Aunt Molly provides a satisfactory solution to Harry's dilemma. Harry also attains some understanding of and sympathy for his father's problem.

I'll Never Love Anything Ever Again, Judy Delton, Ill. by Rodney Pate, Albert Whitman, 1985. Ages 5–8.

When he develops an allergy to dogs, a young boy must part with his beloved dog, Tinsel. The boy poignantly describes Tinsel's good qualities and needs, and the times they've shared. The boy faces the sad separation with support from his mother. *Highly recommended*.

My Book for Kids with Cansur, Jason Gaes, Ill. by Tim and Adam Gaes, Melius and Peterson Pub., 1987. Ages 4–9.

Cancer was discovered in Jason at age six, and he was not expected to live beyond four months. Jason describes the surgery, chemotherapy, and bone marrow tests he endured until remission. This true story, using Jason's own printing and spelling, is an inspirational testimony to conquering fear, pain, and death. This unique autobiography is the only 1987 book included here. *Highly recommended*.

Now One Foot, Now the Other, Tomie de Paola, Putnam, 1981. Ages 4 + .
Bobby's grandfather, Bob, helped him learn how to walk, told him stories, and played special games with him. When Bob suffers a stroke, Bobby endures months of misery. Finally, Bob is able to come home, but the anguish doesn't stop for Bobby until he realizes that it is his turn to help Bob. *Highly recommended*.

Patty Gets Well, Patricia Frevert, photographs by David Jonasson, Creative Education, 1983. Ages 7–10.
Patty Ness tells the inspirational and true story of her fight against leukemia. From diagnosis at age 10, Patty recounts the realities of treatment, her absence from school and from friends, and the struggle for remission of the disease. With the loving care and optimism of her family and doctor, Patty wins the battle.

When Mom or Dad Has Cancer, Carol Lindberg, Ill. by Kathleen Brandl, American Cancer Society, Minnesota Div., 1985. Ages 5–10.
Personally recommended by a young mother who used it to discuss her cancer with her children. David's father has leukemia. At the doctor's office, David meets other children whose parents have cancer. They discuss their feelings, fears, and how the illness has affected their lives. An informative pamphlet about the types of cancer, their treatments, and the ways in which children can cope with this devastating event.

Where's Buddy?, Ron Roy, Ill. by Troy Howell, Clarion, 1982. Ages 7–11.
Buddy, Mike's seven-year-old brother, has diabetes, but he has never accepted responsibility for his illness. When Mike is left to babysit, Buddy disappears. Mike conducts a frantic search, since Buddy must have his insulin or he could die. A good suspense story with lessons about responsibility and health care nicely incorporated.

Dentist

The Dentist and Me, Joy Schaleben-Lewis, photographs by Murray Weiss, Raintree, 1977. O.P. Ages 4–8.
Two children recount their visits to the dentist. Adam has a routine checkup; his teeth are cleaned and X-rayed, and he is taught to care for them. Nikki must have a cavity filled, and this procedure is described. Both narratives emphasize the children's responsibility in caring for their teeth.

Michael and the Dentist, Bernard Wolf, Four Winds Pr., 1980. Ages 4–7.
Michael has been to the dentist before, but this time he has to have a cavity filled. Dr. Schwald explains the mysteries of his dental equipment by giving it magical qualities. Michael is both accepting and skeptical, but he manages to overcome his fear. A nonfiction book that's recommended with reservations because of its simplistic approach.

My Dentist, Harlow Rockwell, Greenwillow, 1975. Ages 2–7.
A trip to the dentist for a routine examination is described by a young girl. She explains the dentist's equipment and his care. The matter-of-fact text, devoid of emotion, is augmented by bright, simple illustrations.

Taryn Goes to the Dentist, Jill Krementz, Crown, 1986. Ages 3–4.
Taryn, age 2½, tells about her first visit to the dentist. The educational and treatment aspects of routine dental care are simply and positively explained for any young child who is about to experience his or her first dental appointment. Despite the book's informational level, the board book format better suits a younger child.

Doctor

The Checkup, Harold Roth, Grosset, 1986. Ages 18 mos.–3 yrs.
Baby goes with Mommy and Daddy to the doctor for a checkup. Engaging photographs and a simple text show the highlights of the visit. A board book for the youngest patient.

A Doctor's Tools, Kenny DeSantis, photographs by Patricia Agre, Dodd, 1985. Ages 4–8.
This book explains 18 different items that are commonly seen and used during a visit to the doctor's office. A nonfiction book that provides answers to many of the questions children may raise. The book's commentary can be used to remove the fear of the unknown.

Going to the Doctor, Fred Rogers, photographs by Jim Judkis, Putnam, 1986. Ages 3–6.
Brightly colored photographs show two young children visiting their doctors. The text provides an accurate depiction of routine health care along with the reassurance that while some things may hurt, others may not. The author's intent is to remove fear of the unknown and to open communication between parents and children. *Highly recommended*.

My Doctor, Harlow Rockwell, Macmillan, 1973. Ages 2–6.
During a visit to his doctor's office, a young boy describes the instruments and equipment he sees and the purpose of each. Examples of a routine physical examination are also explained. Contains bold, colorful

pictures for young children. Older children may require a book that deals more with the emotional impact of the experience.

Your Turn, Doctor, Carla Perez and Deborah Robison, Ill. by Deborah Robison, Dial Pr. Bks., 1982. Ages 5–8.

Gloria is upset about visiting the doctor's office for a checkup. When left alone to calm down, she fantasizes a role reversal in which the doctor becomes the patient, and she forces him to endure the insults, condescension, and discomfort a child may experience during a routine physical. An unusual, humorous approach that acknowledges the anxieties a child may experience.

Emergencies and Accidents

Betsy and the Doctor, Gunilla Wolde, Random, 1978. Ages 4–7.

After Betsy cuts her head at nursery school, she must go to the doctor for stitches. To her amazement, the only pain she suffers is from the shot to numb the area around the cut. Betsy rushes back to tell the story of her adventure to her astonished friends. The subsequent suture removal is also well depicted.

The Emergency Room, Anne and Harlow Rockwell, Macmillan, 1985. Ages 2–5.

A little boy who has sprained his ankle goes to the emergency room. Prosaically, he describes his treatment and his observations in this informational book containing bright, watercolor illustrations. An excellent story to read to young children while waiting in emergency rooms. Recommended for purchase by hospitals.

Emergency Room, Bob and Diane Wolfe, Carolrhoda, 1983. Ages 6–10.

The real-life drama of emergency rooms unfolds in this photo-essay about patients and the experienced professionals who care for them. The treatment needed for minor trauma and illness, and the complex technology and skill required for critical emergencies are explicitly described. A beneficial resource for understanding emergency rooms.

Eric Needs Stitches, Barbara Marino, photographs by Richard Rudinski, Addison-Wesley, 1979. O.P. Ages 5–8.

After a biking accident, Eric goes to the emergency room for stitches. His father calms Eric's fears by explaining what will happen. The book describes events, starting with the father and son's arrival at the hospital to suturing Eric's leg. A sensitive nurse and doctor help Eric cope with this experience.

Hospitalization

The Hospital Book, James Howe, photographs by Mal Warshaw, Crown, 1981. Ages 7–10.

A detailed, nonfiction book depicting the hospitalization of children, from admission to discharge. Children are introduced to the hospital staff and to the procedures and equipment they may encounter. The patient's apprehensions about the experience are supported, and suggestions are given for coping. A reassuring resource to be shared between adult and child.

Hospital Roadmap: A Book to Help Explain the Hospital Experience to Young Children, Ingrid Elliot, Resources Children, 1981. Ages 4–7.

A young girl must go to the hospital for tests because of a stomach problem. To combat the girl's fears, her mother makes a roadmap of the different things she will encounter. Admission procedures, the tests she undergoes, and the surgery of another child are succinctly explained. An adult usage guide is included.

The Hospital Scares Me, Paula Hogan and Kirk Hogan, Ill. by Mary Thelen, Raintree, 1980. Ages 5–9.

Dan falls from the monkey bars, breaking his ankle. A doctor decides that surgery is needed to set the fracture. The initial exam, surgery, and Dan's fears are described. The book's approach is overly dramatic, and children should be told that such extensive treatment and hospitalization are not common for similar injuries.

A Hospital Story: An Open Family Book for Parents and Children Together, Sara B. Stein, photographs by Doris Pinney, Walker and Co., 1974. Ages 4–8.

Jill must have her tonsils removed. Her fears about hospitalization and her parents' efforts to alleviate them are narrated. The author presents two texts, one for young children and the other designed to help adults understand children's perceptions of the experience and answer children's questions. *Highly recommended.*

Jeff's Hospital Book, Harriet Sobol, photographs by Patricia Agre, Walck, 1975. O.P. Ages 4–8.

This nonfiction book tells the story of Jeff, whose eyes have been crossed since birth. Now he's going to have surgery on them. Tests, procedures, and his surgery are described. Jeff's reactions include fear, worry, even boredom, and, finally, joy at going home. Best of all, the final photograph shows Jeff's eyes straightened.

Miffy in the Hospital, Dick Bruna, Price-Stern, 1984. Ages 2–4.

Part of a delightful series about Miffy the rabbit. Miffy's disclosure that her throat hurts prompts a visit to the doctor. From there she is sent to the hospital to have her tonsils removed. A simple story with illustrations, which may allay children's initial fears about hospitalization. For very young children.

Related Titles

Chronic Illness

My Grandma's in a Nursing Home, Judy Delton and Dorothy Tucker.

Chapter 10

Safety Issues

Accidents kill more children between the ages of one and 14 than the next six leading causes combined. Accidents can range from minor trauma to death, and the statistics are shocking. Household accidents account for approximately one-third of all accidental injuries and for one-fifth of all accidental deaths every year. Three thousand children under the age 14 die each year in home accidents.

The tragic fact is that most of these occurrences can be prevented. People who care for children have a vital role in helping them lead safe lives. This goal can be achieved by providing a safe environment, understanding children's cognitive and skill development, and teaching children about potential hazards.

Knowing a child's developmental level can guide adults in making the child's surroundings safe. A child's developmental level also defines what the child needs and can understand in regard to safety instruction. Safety education is enhanced through the use of books, which can be used to gradually build a child's awareness and prevent confusion.

Reading with a child develops a sense of personal safety and stimulates conversation. Books thus can make safety awareness a part of a child's life. Introducing books on a particular subject as it becomes appropriate for the child's needs provides an excellent setting for teaching. For example, when a preschooler learns to open doors and to climb, it becomes necessary to teach the child about the potential hazards of household products. Similarly, the early school-aged child can benefit from reading a book on bike safety.

Caregivers should be warned about the importance of selecting books with a positive focus, otherwise safety rules might take on negative connotations. Many of the directives children hear, especially in their early years, concern safety issues. Nevertheless, awareness of potential hazards can help children lead full, exciting lives as they grow into healthy adults.

Just as parents are inclined to scold or frighten children on this subject, many safety books also tend to be didactic. For this reason, only the best books currently available are included in this chapter.

Bicycles Are Fun to Ride, Dorothy Chlad, Ill. by Lydia Halverson, Childrens Pr., 1984. Ages 4–8.

Mark describes his bicycle and the care it requires, and he clearly explains his rules for safety when riding it. This book stresses that a bike can be great fun, but it requires a responsible owner.

By Yourself, Sara Gilbert, Ill. by Heidi Selig, Lothrop, 1983. Ages 7–12.
An excellent resource, especially for the latchkey child, on being home alone and taking care of oneself. The two chapters on safety include information not found in most other safety books, such as what to do in case of severe weather or electrical failure, and first aid tips.

Dinosaurs, Beware: A Safety Guide, Marc Brown and Stephen Krensky, Little, 1982. Ages 3–6.
Delightful caricatures show dinosaurs dealing with emergency situations and avoiding accidents. This light, humorous approach succeeds in conveying 60 safety tips ranging from not playing with strange animals to the importance of wearing a seat belt. *Highly recommended.*

Matches, Lighters, and Firecrackers Are Not Toys, Dorothy Chlad, Ill. by Lydia Halverson, Childrens Pr., 1982. Ages 3–7.
Jack explains safety rules concerning matches, lighters, firecrackers, and sparklers. Their dangers and appropriate use are described. The book emphasizes that none of these objects are safe for children and should be used only by adults.

On My Own: The Kids' Self-Care Book, Lynette Long, Ill. by JoAnn Hall, Acropolis, 1984. Ages 7–12.
An activity book to prepare children of working parents to care for themselves. Chapters are devoted to games, snacks, and before- and after-school duties. Tips on handling emergencies, fires, intruders, and injuries are also included. All activities are intended to develop safe, responsible self-care. Many of these exercises can be used with younger children as well. Because of the book's format, parents should consider purchasing it rather than borrowing it.

Out to Sea, Anne and Harlow Rockwell, Macmillan, 1980. Ages 6–8. Ready-to-read.
Kate and Jeff discover a deserted old boat and begin to play in it. When the tide comes in, they are washed out to sea. Discovering the children's plight, their anxious parents notify the Coast Guard. Everyone's fears and concerns, and water safety rules are blended in a nondidactic manner into the story of Kate's and Jeff's rescue.

Poisons Make You Sick, Dorothy Chlad, Ill. by Lydia Halverson, Childrens Pr., 1984. Ages 3–7.
Tammy explains the potential poisons in a child's environment. The simple text is augmented by illustrations showing many products that

can be harmful if ingested. Four easy rules are outlined to help children avoid poisoning. Medicines are depicted as poisons, and an explanation of this fallacy is required by the adult reader.

Safety First: Home, Eugene Baker, Ill. by Tom Dunnington, Creative Education, 1980. O.P. Ages 3–8.

Basil the dog and Rover the cat enjoy playing in different rooms of the house. First each room is seen with its potential dangers for accidents, then as clean and safe. Safety First Owl points out hazards and how to correct them in this informational book. Other books in this series include safety tips about water, school, outdoors, fire, and bicycling. Although containing important information, all of the books in this series tend to be pedantic.

Stay Safe, Play Safe: A Book about Safety Rules, Barbara Seuling, Ill. by Kathy Albert, Western, 1985. Ages 4–7.

This book begins with the premise that everyone has a job to do, and children have a duty to their family and friends to keep them safe. Brief sketches of situations that could be dangerous provide examples of how children can help their family and friends stay safe and play safe. As with many safety books, this one tends to sermonize.

That Dog Melly!, Corinne D. Bliss with Austin Bliss, photographs by Corinne D. Bliss and Jim Judkis, Hastings, 1981. Ages 5–8.

Six-year-old Austin's dog, Melly, is older than Austin is, but they are caring companions. Austin describes their special time together and his fright when Melly runs away. Austin does not cross the street, thereby following the rules for his own safety, but lures Melly home.

What to Do When Your Mom or Dad Says. . .Be Prepared!, Joy W. Berry, Childrens Pr., 1981. Ages 5–8.

Humorous cartoons of a brother and sister and their dog illustrate this nonfiction book. The information is very specific in providing exact guidelines to prepare children to handle emergencies. However, the list of medical supplies given has inappropriate recommendations and probably should not have been included.

What Would You Do If. . .? A Safety Guide for You and Your Child, Jeanne Ebert, Ill. by Laurel Porter, Houghton, 1985. Ages 3–8.

Children are invited to play a game of deciding what to do in dangerous situations. Topics included are getting lost, avoiding traffic, and reacting to fire, and handling many other harmful situations. Parents and children are encouraged to agree on a response, then to practice it. This book should be owned rather than borrowed because of its personalized format. *Highly recommended*.

When I Cross the Street, Dorothy Chlad, Ill. by Lydia Halverson, Childrens Pr., 1982. Ages 3–7.

In careful detail, Mary demonstrates and explains her rules for safely crossing the street. Potential hazards, ranging from encountering vehicles to handling certain weather conditions are explored. The safety rules are demonstrated in the girl's hometown and are also depicted in a large city and rural settings.

When There Is a Fire. . . Go Outside, Dorothy Chlad, Ill. by Lydia Halverson, Childrens Pr., 1982. Ages 3–7.

Tony explains what to do in the event of a fire. He describes his family's plan for safety in case of a fire and rules other children should follow if they are involved in such an incident. The book also contains information on firefighters and why they should handle this type of emergency.

Will You Cross Me?, Marilyn Kaye, Ill. by Ned Delaney, Harper, 1985. Ages 6–7. An Early I can read book.

Joe and Sam live on opposite sides of a busy city street and must rely on passersby to help them cross it. Their frustrations in getting together to play ball are humorously described. The safe crossing rule is so ingrained that despite mischance and argument, the boys never venture forth alone.

Chapter 11

Self-Concept/Self-Esteem/ Dealing with Handicaps

Feelings of Inadequacy
General
Multiple Handicaps
Overweight
Speech Problems
Thumbsucking, Bedwetting, Stuttering
Toilet Training
Hearing Impaired
Learning Problems
Mentally Handicapped
Physically Handicapped
Visually Impaired

All children have a basic need to develop a sense of self and to answer the questions: "Who am I?" "How am I like others?" "How am I different?" The search for self-identity is a lifelong process, but it has its roots in early childhood. The struggle is obvious in preschoolers as they vacillate between dependence and independence. As children develop a self-concept, they are able to perceive their personal attributes and limitations and also to understand their individuality.

Children's acceptance of themselves as worthwhile individuals is determined not only in how they see themselves but also in what is reflected by those around them. That is, the attitudes of others are incorporated into children's sense of self-worth. Children should feel valued for their inherent goodness, but often their self-esteem is conditional in that it is dynamically influenced by feedback from peers and adults. Therefore, responses to children, combined with how they compare themselves to others, influence their successes and happiness. If overall their experiences are positive, children can achieve a healthy sense of self-acceptance, which then can be transferred to an acceptance of others for their own value.

A deterrent to the development of sound self-esteem occurs when children see themselves as different from others. Some differences appear more subtle, such as being unathletic or feeling inadequate, while others are more obvious, including physical and mental handicaps. Regardless of the degree of the handicap or problem, it still is significant in that it directly affects children's concept of self-worth.

Regardless of the nature or source of the problem, caregivers can influence how the child copes with it. Attention should be given to children's strengths, and their weaknesses, downplayed. It is important to encourage children to pursue achievements that they can attain, whatever their disabilities. Children need to feel successful. While some problems can be overcome or outgrown, many handicaps are permanent. Children with lifelong disabilities must learn to avoid self-pity and to achieve in areas that fall within their capabilities. As children become aware of their own limitations, their questioning often extends to the differences of other people. It is natural for children to be interested in things that are new or unusual to them. Caregivers can help children develop empathy for and acceptance of people who are dissimilar to themselves.

Whether adults are dealing with a child's own self-concept or a child's acceptance of other people, books can be an invaluable tool in facilitating the process. Books give children the opportunity to understand the concept of self and to observe and identify how people are similar to or different from themselves.

Stories about self-concept, self-esteem, and handicaps can be introduced at various ages, depending on a particular child's needs. Caregivers can offer children exposure to problems such as physical handicaps before such problems are encountered in real life. At other times, books can help answer questions, for example, about mentally handicapped persons. Books and ensuing discussions between adults and children can help to promote empathy for and understanding about people who seem different. Children who themselves experience a problem, such as a hearing impairment or being overweight, can also derive some benefit from identifying with a character who has a similar problem. Books can reassure children and help them understand that they are each special in their own unique way.

The reason for selecting books on a particular topic will determine the approach that is most appropriate for an individual child. It is important that adults appreciate the significance of these concerns as they relate to the child involved. Many stories available today are contrived and do not recognize children's achievements in dealing with a handicap or with feelings of inadequacy. Therefore, some of the books selected for this chapter have shortcomings, and these are noted, but the books were included because of their redeeming qualities. All of the books included in this chapter are intended to enhance children's sense of self-worth.

Feelings of Inadequacy

Arthur's Nose, Marc Brown, Little, 1976. Ages 3–7.

Arthur Anteater worries about his nose because of teasing from his sister and friends. He therefore goes to a rhinologist to have his nose changed. After trying on the noses of various animals, Arthur decides that he is not himself without his particular nose. For everyone who has ever been dissatisfied with a part of their body.

The Biggest Nose, Kathy Caple, Houghton, 1985. Ages 5–7.

Eleanor Elephant is taunted by the other animal children for having the biggest nose in the group and is embarrassed to find out that this is true. When Eleanor tries to shorten her nose, she learns it is good just the way it is. Again confronted, Eleanor finds a way to stop the teasing.

Billy's Shoes, Gen LeRoy, Ill. by J. Winslow Higgenbottom, McGraw-Hill, 1981. Ages 5–8.

Billy believes that he can run fast and jump high because he is wearing his big brother's old shoes. His confidence is lost, however, when his parents force him to wear brand-new shoes. A little dog in danger helps a distraught Billy learn something wonderful about himself.

The Boy with the Special Face, Barbara Girion, Ill. by Heidi Palmer, Abingdon, 1978. O.P. Ages 6–9.

Perry has eyes of a nondescript color, bright red uncontrollable hair, and countless freckles. When a producer comes to his class to find someone for a television commercial, all the children except Perry dress up to display their best attributes. Despite his old clothes and "impossible hairs," Perry wins the job.

But Names Will Never Hurt Me, Bernard Waber, Houghton, 1976. Ages 5–8.

Alison Wonderland is the subject of many jokes because of her name. Confronting her mother, Alsion is assured that the name was given in love and that if she remembers this, no remark will ever hurt her. In a surprise ending, the grown Alison uses her name to her advantage.

Everyone Goes as a Pumpkin, Judith Vigna, Albert Whitman, 1977. Ages 4–7.

Emily has a wonderful Halloween costume, which she loses on her way to her grandmother's. Grandmother suggests that they quickly make a pumpkin costume, but Emily rejects this idea because she wants to be someone special. With her grandmother's help, Emily realizes that a costume is not necessary to make her special.

I Can Do It by Myself, Lessie J. Little and Eloise Greenfield, Ill. by Carole Byard, Crowell, 1978. Ages 5–7.

Donnie is determined to buy a plant by himself for his mother's birthday. Pulling the plant along in his wagon, he feels proud until he encounters a bulldog. Despite crying and falling down, Donnie does not run away and feels a sense of accomplishment as he presents the plant to his mother.

I Hate Red Rover, Joan Lexau, Ill. by Gail Owens, Dutton, 1979. O.P. Ages 5–8.

Every day, Jill's classmates play Red Rover at recess. Jill hates the game and is not good at it, but she hates being laughed at more. Bolstered by encouragement from Grandfather and from a classmate, Jill tries harder, overcomes her animosity for the game, and plays with success.

I Never Win!, Judy Delton, Ill. by Cathy Gilchrist, Carolrhoda, 1981. Ages 5–8.

Charlie never wins at anything. He meets failure in games, contests, and sports. Practicing the piano helps Charlie relieve his frustrations and pays off when he learns that being a winner does not always involve a tangible prize.

I'm Terrific, Marjorie W. Sharmat, Ill. by Kay Chorao. Holiday, 1977. Ages 5–8.

Jason Everett Bear thinks that his admirable traits make him terrific and tells all of his animal friends so. When his self-admiration is not reinforced, Jason becomes sloppy and is nasty to his friends. Unhappy with his own behavior, Jason finally learns that happiness comes from accepting himself.

It's Me, Claudia, Alyse Newman, Watts, 1981. Ages 7–8. An Easy-read story book.

After trying various ways to reduce the ears she hates, Claudia puts on a big, floppy hat to hide them. Wearing the hat has unfortunate consequences: she cannot see or play, and people don't recognize her. After several lonely days, Claudia decides that her ears are not so awful and discards the hat.

It's Not Fair, Charlotte Zolotow, William Pene duBois, Harper, 1976. Ages 5–8.

Martha has long black hair, no freckles, and sings in perfect key. The freckled narrator has curly red hair and can't carry a tune. When Martha reveals that she wants the things her friend despises, the storyteller concludes that it's not fair to either of them. For those who wish that life were different.

Jane, Wishing, Tobi Tobias, Ill. by Trina S. Hyman, Viking, 1977. Ages 5–9.

Jane fantasizes about having a glamorous life, wishing she didn't have straight hair, brown eyes or freckles, and that her name wasn't plain

"Jane." Her family points out the possible problems of Jane's fantasy existence and the advantages of reality. Jane finally decides to accept things
as they are and to be happy. For any dreamer.

Katy Did It, Victoria Boutis, Ill. by Gail Owens, Greenwillow, 1982. Ages
6–10.

Katy, whose previous camping attempts were laughable, is now going
backpacking in the mountains with her father. She is soon disgruntled
by the cold and primitive conditions. Her father, maintaining his humor
and patience, coaxes Katy up the mountain. At the top, Katy realizes that
her achievement far outweighs the hardships.

No Good in Art, Miriam Cohen, Ill. by Lillian Hoban, Greenwillow,
1980. Ages 5–8.

The kindergarten teacher insensitively criticizes Jim's painting. A year
later, as the first grade class eagerly paints for the art teacher, Jim remembers his earlier experience and will not participate. Gentle encouragement from the new teacher and praise from his classmates renew Jim's
confidence in his artistic abilities.

Nobody's Perfect, Not Even My Mother, Norma Simon, Ill. by Dora Leder, Albert Whitman, 1981. Ages 4–8.

One child is good at puzzles, and another at photography. A mother is
a good mechanic, and a father a good bricklayer. Children describe how
these and other achievements are accomplished. In addition the book
also explains that everyone does some things poorly. A light approach to
helping children understand that everyone excels in some things, but nobody is perfect.

Sleeping Ugly, Jane Yolen, Ill. by Diane Stanley, Coward, 1981. Ages 7–8.
A Break-of-day book.

Beautiful Princess Miserella is mean and nasty. Plain Jane is ugly, but
good. A foolish fairy puts them and herself to sleep for 100 years. Prince
Jojo finds them, but decides to practice a kiss on Jane. He falls in love
with her, and Miserella never gets kissed. A humorous, modern fairytale.

So What?, Miriam Cohen, Ill. by Lillian Hoban, Greenwillow, 1982. Ages
5–8.

Jim is plagued with inadequacies. He can't master the monkey bars, his
club fails, and he is the shortest child in the first-grade class. Finally,
Elinor's words "so what" help Jim to understand that his concerns are
trivial and free him to succeed at something.

A Sound to Remember, Sonia Levitin, Ill. by Gabriel Lisowski, Harcourt,
1979. O.P. Ages 6–8.

The villagers mock Jacov, who is slow and clumsy. When he is chosen by the Rabbi to blow the shofar (trumpet) on High Holy Days, Jacov fails miserably and endures taunts from the congregation. The Rabbi acquires another shofar to help Jacov succeed and earn the villagers' respect.

Taking Care of Melvin, Marjorie W. Sharmat, Ill. by Victoria Chess, Holiday, 1980. Ages 4–8.

Melvin the dog is so helpful that his friends take advantage of him. The situation is reversed when Melvin collapses and he makes use of his friends. After doing Melvin's bidding all day, the friends rebel. Melvin and his friends discover that he is much happier when he is taking care of himself, not others.

Too Short Fred, Susan Meddaugh, Houghton, 1978. O.P. Ages 5–8.

This book's beginning reader format features five stories about Fred, the cat, who is much shorter than his friends. Themes include Fred's winning a race and outwitting a bully. In each story, Fred seems to be at a disadvantage because of his height, but he triumphs due to his cleverness or luck.

Willy the Wimp, Anthony Browne, Knopf, 1984. Ages 5–8.

Willy, a chimpanzee, apologizes whenever someone runs into him, but soon he is tired of being bullied and called a wimp. After months of a strenuous physical fitness regimen, the mere sight of Willy causes the bullies to run. However, when Willy runs headlong into a pole, he reverts to his timorous self.

General

Liking Myself, Pat Palmer, Ill. by Betty L. Shondeck, Impact Pubs., 1977. Ages 5–9.

An excellent introduction to the topics of feelings, self-esteem, and acceptance of others. The concepts are simply explained, and children are given ways to talk about and analyze their own feelings. Due to the book's format, purchase is suggested. *The Mouse, the Monster, and Me*, a book on assertiveness by the same author, is also recommended for children aged 8–12.

Multiple Handicaps

My Friend Leslie: The Story of a Handicapped Child, Maxine B. Rosenberg, photographs by George Ancona, Lothrop, 1983. Ages 5–8.

Karin describes her friend, Leslie, who is multi-handicapped. Despite her visual and hearing impairments and extremity motor problems, Leslie enjoys the activities of kindergarten with a little help from Karin, the teacher, and her classmates. She is a determined youngster with a wonderful sense of humor. *Highly recommended*.

Someone Special, Just like You, Tricia Brown, photographs by Fran Ortiz, Holt, 1982. Ages 3–7.

Preschool children with physical, mental, and sensory disabilities are depicted swimming, playing, and learning, in black-and-white photographs. In brief words, the text shows that it is not their differences, but rather their similarities that make all children special.

Overweight

Don't Call Me Fatso, Barbara Philips, Ill. by Helen Cogancherry, Raintree, 1980. Ages 5–9.

Rita feels humiliated and self-conscious when her classmates tease her about being fat. Her parents acknowledge her problem, and together they exercise and diet. Rita has difficulty with the new regimen, but her sacrifices are finally rewarded. Although addressing a significant problem, the book greatly oversimplifies the resolution.

Dumb Old Casey Is a Fat Tree, Barbara Bottner, Harper, 1979. Ages 7–10.

Patrick undermines Casey's dream of being a ballet dancer by telling her she's too fat. In dance class, the prima donnas make her feel inferior. But Casey perseveres, and her devotion to ballet brings her a greater reward than being a star can. A special story on the benefits of hard work. *Highly recommended*.

Speech Problems

Growl When You Say R, Muriel Stanek, Ill. by Phil Smith, Albert Whitman, 1979. Ages 5–8.

When Robbie starts a new school, he is teased because of his impaired speech. He feels self-conscious and lonely. With help in a special speech class and with hard work, Robbie is able to overcome his problem and make friends. Contains a somewhat contrived plot, but the book offers hopeful support for those who suffer from this common disorder.

Thumbsucking, Bedwetting, Stuttering

Danny and His Thumb, Kathryn F. Ernst, Ill. by Tomie de Paola, Prentice-Hall, 1973. Ages 4–7.

Danny like to suck his thumb. Whether waiting for someone, riding in the car, or just thinking, sucking his thumb gives Danny great pleasure. However, after he starts school, thumbsucking does not provide the same satisfaction. Many new activities occupy Danny's time, and gradually he does not miss sucking him thumb. *Highly recommended.*

David Decides about Thumbsucking: A Motivating Story for Children; An Informative Guide for Parents, Susan M. Heitler, photographs by Paula Singer, Reading Matters, 1985. Ages 5–7.

In this nonfiction book, David tells why he sucks his thumb. After talking about this practice with his brother, sister, and parents, David decides to quit. With his parents' support and help, David gains confidence so that he can conquer his habit. Extensive parent section included.

Don't Worry Dear, Joan Fassler, Ill. by Stuart Kranz, Human Sci. Pr., 1971. Ages 4–7.

Toddler Jenny suffers the agonies of childhood. She wets the bed, stutters, and sucks her thumb. Through it all, her mother comforts Jenny and gently reassures her that the problem will resolve. An excellent contribution on common problems that concern children and their parents. This fine book has mesmerized storytime groups. *Highly recommended.*

Toilet Training

Going to the Potty, Fred Rogers, photographs by Jim Judkis, Putnam, 1986. Ages 2–4.

A nonfiction book about toilet training, depicting the growth of children from dependent infants to toddlers learning new skills. Colorful photographs show children getting acquainted with the bathroom and starting to use a potty chair and toilet. A book that's reassuring to parents and children alike on infants' slow but sure progress from wearing diapers to staying dry.

Sam's Potty, Barbro Lindgren, Ill. by Eva Eriksson, Morrow, 1986. Ages 2–4.

Sam doesn't like his "potty." He tries making his dog sit on it, but doggie falls off. So Sam demonstrates its use and is proud of the results. Humorous illustrations and few words successfully capture Sam's accomplishment for the inspiration of the book's intended age group.

Hearing Impaired

Anna's Silent World, Bernard Wolf, Lippincott, 1977. Ages 6–10.

A photo-documentary of the life of a six-year-old named Anna, who is deaf. Because of four years of extensive therapy and determined effort, Anna is able to go to school with children of normal hearing. By using her hearing aids and by lip reading, Anna leads an active life, including taking dancing lessons.

A Button in Her Ear, Ada B. Litchfield, Ill. by Eleanor Mill, Albert Whitman, 1976. Ages 5–9.

Angela has problems at home and at school because she cannot hear correctly what is being said. Her parents take her to medical specialists, who diagnose her hearing loss, and she gets a hearing aid. The "magic button" is accepted willingly by Angela with the support of her parents and teachers.

I Can't Always Hear You, Joy Zelonky, Ill. by Barbara Bejna and Shirlee Jensen, Raintree, 1980. Ages 6–10.

After attending a school for the hearing-impaired, Kim enters a regular school. The children's teasing compounds her anxieties about being different. Kim is ready to quit when the principal, who shares her problem, gives her practical advice that helps. A helpful book, but the last pages in which her classmates describe their "differences" mar the story.

I Can't Hear like You, Althea, Ill. by Jean Anderson, Dinosaur Pubs., 1985. Ages 4–8.

The young narrator cannot hear well. His hearing aids magnify voices, but also increase other noises. Listening can be exhausting because the hearing aids must be augmented by lip reading and watching facial expressions. This simple account shows a child meeting the challenges of his hearing impairment with acceptance and fortitude.

(R) *I Have a Sister, My Sister Is Deaf*, Jeanne W. Peterson, Ill. by Deborah Ray, Harper, 1977. Ages 4–8.

A young girl describes the positive and negative elements in her deaf sister's life. Her sister cannot hear the phone ringing or be awakened by thunder. The narrator emphasizes that although being deaf doesn't hurt, her sister's feelings do when people don't understand her problem. The text and illustrations provide a warm, tender portrayal of a sister's love.

I'm Deaf and It's Okay, Lorraine Aseltine and Evelyn Mueller, Ill. by Helen Cogancherry, Albert Whitman, 1986. Ages 5–8.

When a young deaf boy realizes that he will always have to wear hearing aids, he rebels. A deaf teenager visiting his school helps the boy understand that he can have an active adult life. The plot is simplistic but provides a good depiction of the fears, frustrations, and satisfactions of the hearing impaired.

Jamie's Tiger, Jan Wahl, Ill. by Tomie de Paola, Harcourt, 1978. Ages 4–8.

After contracting the German measles, Jamie can no longer hear. He withdraws with only a stuffed tiger to comfort him. Slowly, with the help of family, professionals, and friends, a lonely Jamie finds happiness, and his tiger no longer growls. Although the story may seem outdated because German measles can now be prevented, Jamie's story is supportive for all hearing-impaired children. *Highly recommended.*

What Is the Sign for Friend?, Judith E. Greenberg, photographs by Gayle Rothschild, Watts, 1985. Ages 6–8.
  This nonfiction book describes the life of Shane, who was born deaf. He goes to a regular school but receives speech therapy and has a signer in the classroom. Outside school, Shane enjoys biking, swimming, playing soccer, and doing other activities with his hearing friends.

Words in Our Hands, Ada B. Litchfield, Ill. by Helen Cogancherry, Albert Whitman, 1980. Ages 6–9.
  Nine-year-old Michael describes life with his sisters and their deaf parents. Until the family's move to a new town, things aren't bad. But in addition to the adjustment of moving, the children must now cope with the awareness of having parents who are different. The book has a contrived plot but is a good introduction to hearing impairment.

Learning Problems

The Beast in Ms. Rooney's Room, Patricia R. Giff, Ill. by Blanche Sims, Dell, 1984. Ages 6–9.
  Richard Best, the story's "Beast," is repeating second grade. Telling his old classmates it's all a mistake, Richard doesn't want to make friends in his new class or attend special reading classes. Taunted by former classmates, Richard strives to win the school banner for Ms. Rooney's room, thus acquiring new friends and discovering the joy of reading.

Different, Not Dumb, Margot Marek, photographs by Barbara Kirk, Watts, 1985. Ages 6–8.
  Mike is a second-grader who has trouble reading. Sometimes he feels dumb, especially when he has to go to a special teacher for reading. Mike learns a different way of looking at words from her, which he and his friend Jeff use to prevent an accident. The boys become heroes.

The Flunking of Joshua T. Bates, Susan Shreve, Ill. by Diane De Groat, Knopf, 1984. Ages 7–10.
  Joshua struggles with the injustice of repeating third grade and with the taunts of his former classmates. He vacillates between fantasies of running away or of being promoted. Mrs. Goodwin, his new teacher, treats Joshua with respect and provides tutoring. With effort, Joshua achieves promotion but sadly discovers that he will miss Mrs. Goodwin. *Highly recommended.*

Frankie Is Staying Back, Ron Roy, Ill. by Walter Kessell, Clarion, 1981. Ages 7–10.

When Frankie learns that he will have to repeat third grade, he and his best friend, Jonas, argue. Jonas' plan to avoid separation deepens the misunderstanding. Forced to analyze his behavior, Jonas mends the quarrel with Frankie and offers a plausible solution. The story incorporates a valuable lesson on the importance of expressing feelings.

Jamie's Turn, Jamie DeWitt, Ill. by Julie Brinckloe, Raintree, 1984. Ages 6–10.

Jamie is eleven when his stepfather, Butch, is hurt on a tractor. In the following year, while Butch endures numerous operations, Jamie has responsibility for doing the farm work. The final page of this true story reveals that Jamie has a learning disability. A beautifully illustrated tale of inspiration and achievement for children with learning problems.

Mentally Handicapped

Jon O.: A Special Boy, Elaine Ominsky, photographs by Dennis Simonetti, Prentice-Hall, 1977. O.P. Ages 4–8.

Jon O. has Down syndrome. His difficulties in learning simple things at home and at school are described, as are his special joys. It takes Jon O. a long time to learn his colors, but he also sings the loudest at birthday parties. A loving portrayal accompanied by outstanding black-and-white photographs. *Highly recommended*.

Like Me, Alan Brightman, Little, 1976. Ages 5–8.

The words of a young mentally retarded boy, recorded here, define the label of "retarded" and explain that all children and their emotional needs have a common ground. This book stresses that the difference between the retarded and other people is truly in the eyes of the beholder. Color photographs highlight the text.

Making Room for Uncle Joe, Ada B. Litchfield, Ill. by Gail Owens, Albert Whitman, 1984. Ages 6–9.

Uncle Joe has Down syndrome and comes to live temporarily with his sister's family. His nephew, Dan, describes the family's apprehensions and their stressful adjustments. Joe eventually becomes a part of the family, and they ask him to stay. A simplistic tale, but it effectively deals with some stereotypes about mentally handicapped adults.

More Time to Grow: Explaining Mental Retardation to Children: A Story, Sharon H. Grollman, Ill. by Arthur Polonsky, Beacon, 1977. O.P. Ages 6–10.

Carla has just found out that her five-year-old brother, Arthur, is retarded. Carla is angry and embarrassed until Arthur's simple joy in living makes her realize her love for him. Includes an extensive adult section. A sensitive contribution that can help siblings understand their emotional reactions to mental retardation.

My Friend Jacob, Lucille Clifton, Ill. by Thomas DiGrazia, Dutton, 1980. Ages 5–8.

Sam is eight, and his friend Jacob, who is mentally handicapped, is 17. Sam describes how they help each other and shares Jacob's triumphs, including learning to knock on a door. A heart-warming story of an unusual friendship with a special bond.

My Sister, Karen Hirsch, Ill. by Nancy Inderleden, Carolrhoda, 1977. O.P. Ages 5–8.

A young boy tenderly describes his older sister, who is retarded. Sometimes he is angry when she gets more attention from his parents or when their family outings are spoiled by people's reactions to her. But his sister is also gentle, kind, and full of joy, and he loves her just the way she is.

My Sister Is Different, Betty R. Wright, Ill. by Helen Cogancherry, Raintree, 1981. Ages 5–8.

Carlo is responsible for Terry, his mentally retarded older sister, and he bitterly resents it. When Terry gets lost in the store while he is caring for her, Carlo suddenly remembers all her loving qualities. After Terry is found, Carlo has a new realization of his love for her. A simplistic but adequate treatment.

My Sister's Special, Jo Prall, photographs by Linda Gray, Childrens Pr., 1985. Ages 4–8.

A young boy describes his sister Angie, who has "brain damage." She cannot walk, talk, or use her arms or hands, but she can laugh. Angie goes to school and is learning to communicate through a language board. Black-and-white photographs accompany this loving portrait of Angie.

Stay Away from Simon!, Carol Carrick, Ill. by Donald Carrick, Clarion, 1985. Ages 7–10.

On Martha's Vineyard in the 1830s, Lucy and her younger brother, Josiah, become lost in a snowstorm while walking home from school. A mentally handicapped boy whom they fear and try to avoid rescues them despite their reluctance to go with him. An excellent book for helping children understand others who seem different. *Highly recommended.*

Physically Handicapped

About Handicaps: An Open Family Book for Parents and Children Together, Sara B. Stein, photographs by Dick Frank, Walker, 1974 (pap. 1984). Ages 5–8.

Matthew's obsession with his crooked toe symbolizes his fear of handicaps. He behaves with callousness toward Joe, who has cerebral palsy, and is terrified of a man with a hook arm. With his father's help, Matthew gradually faces his fears and develops a special bond with Joe. Adult text included.

The Balancing Girl, Berniece Rabe, Ill. by Lillian Hoban, Dutton, 1981. Ages 5–8.

Margaret is good at balancing objects, whether she's in her wheelchair or on crutches. However, her rival, Tommy, trivializes all her efforts. When Margaret works on a project for the school carnival that raises the most money, even Tommy acknowledges her achievement. Margaret's disability is incidental to the story's plot.

Captain Hook, That's Me, Ada B. Litchfield, Ill. by Sonia Lisker, Walker, 1982. Ages 7–10.

Judy is a vivacious, fun-loving girl, undaunted by the hook that is her left hand. Her confidence is shaken, however, when her father announces they must move. She worries about being accepted by her new classmates. After the move, Judy finds not only new friends but also the chance to fulfill a dream.

Don't Feel Sorry for Paul, Bernard Wolf, Lippincott, 1974. Ages 7–10.

Paul, age seven, was born with incomplete hands and feet, and must wear three prosthetic devices. Paul's active life and the emotional impact of his handicaps are described in this photo-documentary. Because of hard work and determination, Paul not only rides a bike and a horse; he also wins a medal in a horse show. *Highly recommended*.

It's Okay to Look at Jamie, Patricia D. Frevert, photographs by David Jonasson, Creative Education, 1983. O.P. Ages 7–10.

Eleven-year-old Jamie wears leg braces because she has spina bifida. With the support of family and friends, gutsy Jamie runs a 50-yard dash and endures frequent, sometimes painful medical evaluations. A true story about Jamie's efforts to lead a normal life while coping with her disability.

Nick Joins In, Joe Lasker, Albert Whitman, 1980. Ages 6–8.

Nick is anxious about going to school. Since being confined to a wheelchair, he has been taught at home. Entering a regular school, he now must deal with the curiosity of the other children. Nick and his classmates learn their commonalities, and in a contrived ending, he earns his place among his peers even though he's disabled.

Our Teacher's in a Wheelchair, Mary E. Powers, Albert Whitman, 1986. Ages 4–7.

Brian Hanson became a paraplegic when an accident occurred during a lacrosse game. Despite his disability, Brian enjoys teaching at a day-care center and being independent. The children learn that paralysis is not contagious, as their teacher helps and educates them. In a nonfiction photo-essay, Brian demonstrates the challenges of caring for himself and others.

Rajesh, Curt and Gita Kaufman, photographs by Curt Kaufman, Atheneum, 1985. Ages 5–8.

Rajesh was born missing both legs and part of his right hand. He dreads starting kindergarten because he's afraid others will laugh at him. By the end of the year, Rajesh's classmates learn to appreciate his differences. Rajesh overcomes his self-consciousness and realizes that he can do most things his friends can.

Ride the Red Cycle, Harriette G. Robinet, Ill. by David Brown, Houghton, 1980. Ages 6–10.

More than anything else, eleven-year-old Jerome wants to ride a "cycle." Everyone thinks Jerome's dream is impossible because he is physically handicapped and can't even walk. His irascible nature and stubbornness, together with family support, help Jerome achieve his dream and more.

Thinking Big, Susan Kuklin, Lothrop, 1986. Ages 6–9.

Jaime Osborn is an active, optimistic dwarf. She attends a regular school and lives with her normal-sized family. When Jamie initially meets her best friend, she congratulates him on knowing his first dwarf. Jaime has triumphed over her difficulties by learning to think big. A nonfiction book.

Visually Impaired

® *Arthur's Eyes*, Marc Brown, Little, 1979. Ages 4–8.

Arthur Anteater has trouble reading and playing sports. He sees better after his parents get him glasses. When Arthur's friends mock him, he decides he can do without glasses. After Arthur has several misadventures, his teacher convinces him to change his mind. Finally, Francine, Arthur's biggest tormentor, decides that glasses are glamorous.

A Bowl of Sun, Frances Wosmek, Childrens Pr., 1976. O.P. Ages 6–9.

Megan is blind, but she flourishes in her father's, Mike's, love. They work together in a leather shop and enjoy their life by the ocean. When Mike moves them to Boston for Megan's schooling, she becomes despondent. However, her zest for life is renewed through the creation of a gift inspired by Mike and Megan's past.

A Cane in Her Hand, Ada B. Litchfield, Ill. by Eleanor Mill, Albert Whitman, 1977. Ages 5–8.

Valerie's failing vision necessitates changes in her life. At school, Valerie meets with a special teacher who helps her depend on her other senses and use a cane. Although frustrated, Valerie strives to accept the cane for the freedom it brings. The book has a contrived plot but is noteworthy for its constructive approach.

Cromwell's Glasses, Holly Keller, Greenwillow, 1982. Ages 4–7.

Cromwell is nearsighted and botches everything he tries. His brother and sister criticize and mock him. New glasses finally help Cromwell see, but he hates them because of the other children's teasing. His sister finally intervenes and gives Cromwell the chance to show his talents while wearing his glasses.

Patrick, Yes You Can, Patricia D. Frevert, photographs by Sally D. Martini, Creative Education, 1983. O.P. Ages 7–12.

After struggling with glaucoma since birth, Patrick becomes totally blind at age eight. Once active and sports-minded, Patrick now does not think he can return to his school. His father tells him, "yes, you can." Now, four years later, Patrick is on the honor roll, plays sports, and enjoys a healthy social life.

See You Tomorrow, Charles, Miriam Cohen, Ill. by Lillian Hoban, Greenwillow, 1983. Ages 5–8.

The first-graders try to protect their new classmate, Charles, because he is blind. They acknowledge his small accomplishments and recognize that he might be sad. During recess one day, the children sneak into a dark basement and are scared. Charles leads them to safety, and his friends develop a new respect for him. *Highly recommended*.

The Seeing Stick, Jane Yolen, Ill. by Remy Charlip and Demetra Maraslis, Crowell, 1977. Ages 6–10.

Princess Huei Ming is blind, so her father, the emperor, offers a fortune in jewels to anyone who can help her. Many people try, but all fail, until a tattered old man with a long walking stick and a whittling knife teaches the princess to see with her fingers. Contains beautiful illustrations.

Ⓡ *Through Grandpa's Eyes*, Patricia MacLachlan, Ill. by Deborah Pay, Harper, 1979. Ages 5–8.

When John is at his grandparent's, he does everything with Grandpa. They exercise, play the cello, and go for walks. John has learned to view the world as his blind grandfather does, even to see the smile in his grandmother's voice. Warm illustrations accompany this tender story. *Highly recommended*.

Watch Out, Ronald Morgan!, Patricia R. Giff, Ill. by Susanna Natti, Viking, 1985. Ages 5–8.

Ronald Morgan is convinced that with his new glasses, he'll be a superkid. When he still mixes up the pet food and can't throw straight, he decides the glasses don't work. His sensitive teacher boosts Ronald's faltering ego and makes him realize that consistent practice and wearing the glasses will help him perform better.

Related Titles

Feelings of Inadequacy

The Candy Corn Contest, Patricia R. Giff.

Jim Meets the Thing, Miriam Cohen.

The 329th Friend, Majorie W. Sharmat.

Tramp, Malcolm Carrick.

Willy the Champ, Anthony Browne.

Visually Impaired

The Gift, Helen Coutant.

Chapter 12

Sexual Equality

Sexual stereotypes, passed down from generation to generation, become indelibly etched in children's minds and usually are accepted without question by the time they become adults. These stereotypes are invariably based on the traditional American household, which is typically characterized by men being the unemotional, brave, and logical breadwinners, and women serving as the passive, dependent, and nurturing homemakers.

Today, social attitudes and economic trends are changing the assumptions about gender capabilities, roles, and needs that govern our lives, but the transition is slow and often painful. For many people, inflexible thinking prevents the understanding that both men and women are capable of roles and attitudes not traditionally recognized.

As females continue to become more assertive and men more nurturing, it becomes clearer that specific emotions and feelings, traits, and roles are not the possession of a particular sex; human characteristics are not assigned on the basis of gender. The ideal image for men and women needs to be one of "humanness."

As early as infancy, gender critically influences how others react to children. Furthermore, preschoolers' love of books at a time when they are most impressionable influences their socialization. Preschoolers also have an affinity for requesting books to be read over and over again, which further enhances the impressions they receive through this medium. Through the stereotyped images presented in stories and pictures, boys and girls learn of their differences, not only physically, but also how they should act, feel, and value things.

Additionally, the mass media subject children to a steady barrage of messages that define what a male or female should be like. For instance, TV personalities play stereotyped roles in shows and commercials. Family life is portrayed with a high percentage of middle-class families living in the suburbs, complete with dad as an executive and mom as the primary caretaker of the children.

By school age, children already are fitting into gender stereotypes. In the elementary years, boys and girls progress through countless reading lessons, learning not only basic reading skills, but also about life in general. These stories and pictures may reinforce the stereotypic behavior of men and women. This reinforcement further narrows children's perceptions of the choices they have open to them and of what they can one day hope to achieve.

Interestingly, sex role stereotyping may be implicated in the reading difficulties of some boys, who might lack the motivation to succeed in reading because it is perceived by them as a feminine activity. On the other hand, role models for girls' achievements are sparse. There are few stories about women who are competent and assertive. This persistent indoctrination can result in children who refuse to accept activities related to the opposite gender. More books are needed for children that show women and men who are accepting new responsibilities.

Adults can help boys and girls sort out what they see, hear, and read so that they can avoid a destiny limited by sexually stereotyped roles. Children are not usually able to analyze behavior and judge it accurately. They may accept it without question if they are not helped to form or change their attitudes and to understand how they and their peers feel about sex role stereotypes. Boys and girls need no longer reject opportunities because of their sex. Girls can excel in sports and leadership, and boys can find new fulfillment in dance and nurturing.

Adults should take care to encourage and support children in their achievements as well as to provide chances for them to develop new skills and characteristics. Children may need help in coping with the reactions of their own parents, other adults, and peers as they pursue activities that their same-sex friends do not enjoy. From an early age, children can use books as an important part of their role development in the socialization process. Stories also can reinforce the role modeling provided by parents and others in children's expanding social environment.

Books can expose children to both traditional and nontraditional options. Through books, children can explore the total range of human feelings, skills, roles, and emotions. Children can also learn that a wide range of emotions and feelings is acceptable for both boys and girls.

The boundaries imposed by sexual stereotyping can be broken down when caregivers and children read books that focus on this subject. Discussion between adults and children about these stories can help children confront their biases and test them against reality. Reading is a safe way for children to move beyond the limits of traditional gender-related behaviors and roles. Books can help children understand that they can maintain their sexual identity yet choose options previously assigned to the other sex.

As parents and other adults choose books that deal with gender stereotyping to share with children, it is important to be selective. The current literature still tends to promote preparation for traditional roles. Most available stories show men as risk-takers and providers who are active and clever, while women do little of anything that is interesting. Women in these stories rely on men for intervention in problem solving and perform traditionally female occupations.

Although useful for confronting other problems, fairytales continue to reinforce the concept of men being brave and independent, while women are beautiful and passive or cast as the wicked witch. Mythical tales and nursery rhymes further support the stereotyping of sexes. In these stories, young girls achieve happiness through marriage to Prince Charming, while boys are encouraged to seek recognition through competence and independence.

Today, society somewhat encourages people to advance beyond the confinement of roles previously prescribed, but children's literature is slow to reflect this trend. Many of the books written as antidotes to sexual stereotyping may actually promote it because they are so blatant in trying to represent a liberated viewpoint. A limited number of quality books that address the issue of sexual stereotyping are available. Some of these have a subtle message, such as *Willy the Champ*, while others, including *Everybody Knows That*, are more direct. The best of both types available have been included in this chapter.

Arthur's Pen Pal, Lillian Hoban, Harper, 1976. Ages 6–8. An I am reading book.

Arthur thinks he would like to be his pen pal's brother because he would have a partner for karate. His little sister, Violet, gets hurt too easily and is no fun. To his amazement, Arthur learns that his pen pal is a girl and decides that Violet is not so bad after all.

Backyard Basketball Superstar, Monica Klein, Ill. by Nola Langner, Pantheon, 1981. Ages 6–8. An I am reading book.

As captain of the Flyers, Jeremy is chagrined to discover that his little sister wants to try out for his basketball team. Seeing Melanie play, however, Jeremy knows that she is cut out to be a superstar. Jeremy battles his stereotyped opinions about girls as well as his feelings of sibling rivalry, and Melanie makes the team when Jeremy's sense of fairness triumphs.

Daddy Makes the Best Spaghetti, Anna G. Hines, Clarion, 1986. Ages 3–6.

Corey's father picks him up from day care, then they shop and make dinner. The spaghetti is ready when Mommy returns from work. After eating, Corey and Mommy clean the kitchen. Then Daddy appears as "Bathman" and flies Corey to the tub. An excellent choice for its absence of stereotyping in describing family responsibilities.

Deborah Sampson Goes to War, Bryna Stevens, Ill. by Florence Hill, Carolrhoda, 1984. Ages 6–9.

Gifted with strength, the ability to read, and a sympathy for the colonists, Deborah Sampson decides to become a soldier during the American Revolution. Disguised as a man and calling herself Robert Shurtleff, she fights for two years undiscovered. A simple historical account that offers a strong role model for girls.

Everett Anderson's Friend, Lucille Clifton, Ill. by Ann Grifalconi, Holt, 1976. O.P. Ages 4–8.

Everett is looking forward to meeting the new people in his apartment building. When he finally does, he is disappointed because "it's a family of girls." Worse yet, one of them can run well and beat him at baseball. When Everett forgets his apartment key one day, he overcomes his prejudice against girls and makes a friend.

Everybody Knows That!, Susan Pearson, Ill. by Diane Paterson, Dial, 1978. O.P. Ages 5–8.

Patty and Herbie are best friends and play everything together, from cars to dolls. Their kindergarten classmates Mickey and Jason tell them that some activities are for boys, others for girls. After being banished from the boys' play, Patty excludes Herbie from cookie making, and he experiences the frustration of role stereotyping. *Highly recommended*.

Helga's Dowry: A Troll Love Story, Tomie de Paola, Harcourt, 1977. Ages 5–9.

Spurned by her suitor, Helga, the troll, decides to earn a dowry for herself. Because of her cleverness and hard work, Helga acquires riches. She also realizes that she wants to be loved for what she is, not for what she has. In a surprise ending, Helga marries the king. Contains delightful, humorous illustrations.

Just like Daddy, Frank Asch, Prentice-Hall, 1981. O.P. Ages 2–6.

A little bear does everything just like his daddy. He gets up, dresses, and offers his mother a flower, all in the fashion of his father. As the family fishes, the similarities end when little bear catches a big fish "just like Mommy." A storytime favorite.

The Little Jewel Box, Marianna Mayer, Ill. by Margot Tomes, Dial Pr. Bks., 1986. Ages 5–9.

A humorous modern fairytale about the adventures of Isabel. Plagued by misfortune, Isabel is rescued by the men in the little jewel box whenever she's in danger of death. After both her husband and her jewel box disappear, they are restored through Isabel's tenacity and kindness. A strong female heroine.

A Man Can Be . . ., Susan Kempler and Doreen Rappaport, photographs by Russell Dian, Human Sci. Pr., 1984. Ages 4–8.

A nonfiction book depicting the many facets of a man's personality. Black-and-white photographs of a father with his son demonstrate different characteristics, from being a loving parent to needing time alone. Provides excellent insights instead of the usual male stereotypes.

The Man Who Kept House, retold by Kathleen and Michael Hague, Ill. by Michael Hague, Harcourt, 1981. Ages 5–8.
A farmer belittles his wife's housework until she suggests that they trade places. While she works the fields, disasters befall him. She returns to find the cow hanging off the roof and her husband in the cooking pot. His derision turns to respect. Illustrations capture the humor of this folktale.

® *Max*, Rachel Isadora, Macmillan, 1976. Ages 4–8.
Max plays baseball every week, and he is great. One Saturday, he accompanies his sister to her dance class. While watching, Max is irresistibly drawn to the routines. Despite his waiting team, Max must dance! Now every Saturday before his baseball game, Max goes to dance class. A book that dispels gender role stereotypes. *Highly recommended*.

My Daddy Don't Go to Work, Madeena S. Nolan, Ill. by Jim LaMarche, Carolrhoda, 1978. Ages 5–8.
A young girl's father cannot find work despite looking every day. She loves having him cook the meals and play with her after school. Discouraged, he decides to go away to seek employment, but his wife and daughter persuade him that they must stay together. A poignant tale of family unity triumphing over stereotypes.

My Mommy Makes Money, Joyce S. Mitchell, Ill. by True Kelley, Little, 1984. Ages 5–8.
In picture book format, a variety of nontraditional occupations for women are presented. A single-page description of each job is given, accompanied by illustrations of a woman so employed. Careers range from car salesperson to paperhanger, from surgeon to minister.

Oliver Button Is a Sissy, Tomie de Paola, Harcourt, 1979. Ages 4–8.
Oliver Button prefers reading, drawing, and dancing to playing ball. The boys tease him for being a sissy, but the girls defend him. His parents send him to dancing school, and Oliver's hard work and determination pay off in unexpected acclaim. For all children struggling against stereotyped roles. *Highly recommended*.

Piggybook, Anthony Browne, Knopf, 1986. Ages 5–8.
In addition to going to work, Mrs. Piggott does all the cooking, washing, and cleaning for her demanding husband and two sons. When she disappears, they literally turn into pigs. After fending for themselves,

the three are willing to share family responsibilities upon Mrs. Piggott's return. A hilarious satire.

Rachel and Obadiah, Brinton Turkle, Dutton, 1978. Ages 5–8.
Rachel and Obadiah, young Quakers, learn that they can earn money for carrying the news of a ship arriving at Nantucket. Obadiah scoffs at the idea of a girl running fast enough for such a task. Humiliated and surprised when she runs faster than him, he finds his sister both capable and generous. Helpful in understanding sexual stereotypes.

Ⓡ *Sam Johnson and the Blue Ribbon Quilt*, Lisa C. Ernst, Lothrop, 1983. Ages 5–8.
When Sam Johnson discovers that he likes sewing, he tries to join his wife's quilting club. He is rejected, so he organizes one for the men. The competition between the two factions culminates when they both have their quilts ruined on the way to the fair. Together they work to produce a prize-winning quilt.

Someday with My Father, Helen E. Buckley, Ill. by Ellen Eagle, Harper, 1985. Ages 4–8.
A girl dreams about the adventures she will enjoy with her father. She envisions their enjoyment of outdoor activities and her father's compliments on her expertise. Because of a cast on her leg, the time has not yet come for these experiences, but father and daughter still find delight in each other.

That's Enough for One Day, J.P.!, Susan Pearson, Ill. by Kay Chorao, Dial, 1977. O.P. Ages 5–8.
After several days of reading, John Philip's mother chases him outside. Everything he does makes her holler. He hits a home run through a window and dumps paint on the neighbor's roses. By lunchtime, both have had enough. J.P. is delighted to be confined to his room and to continue reading.

Tough Eddie, Elizabeth Winthrop, Ill. by Lillian Hoban, Dutton, 1985. Ages 4–7.
Eddie feels and acts like a tough kid, so he is furious when his sister tells his best friends about his dollhouse. Their friendship appears to be ruined until Eddie's brave reaction to a bee renews their admiration. A humorous story for all children struggling with sex-role stereotyping.

When We Grow Up, Anne Rockwell, Dutton, 1981. Ages 3–7.
In picture book format, a young boy describes the aspirations of his classmates. Emily wants to be an astronaut, and Nancy a plumber. Ned wants a career as an artist, while the narrator wants to be a teacher. An

excellent, simple exposure to several occupational opportunities unrestricted by gender.

William's Doll, Charlotte Zolotow, Ill. by William Pene DuBois, Harper, 1972. Ages 4–8.

William wants a doll to care for and love. His brother calls this idea creepy, the neighbor boy says he's a sissy, and his father brings him other toys. William's grandmother understands and buys him the perfect doll. She knows it will help him practice to be a good father. *Highly recommended*.

Willy the Champ, Anthony Browne, Knopf, 1985. Ages 5–8.

Willy likes to read and listen to music. Although he tries, he isn't good at sports. When he cries in movies, everyone laughs. One day, Willy inadvertently bests the neighborhood bully in a fight. He is declared a champ. The final page shows Willy reading in a levitated chair.

Related Titles

Abby, Jeanette Caines.

Best Friends for Frances, Russell Hoban.

Blackberries in the Dark, Mavis Jukes.

I'll Tell on You, Joan Lexau.

Mandy's Grandmother, Liesel M. Skorpen.

My Mom Got a Job, Lucia B. Smith.

Sarah, Plain and Tall, Patricia MacLachlan.

The Terrible Thing That Happened at Our House, Marge Blaine.

Chapter 13

Understanding Society

General
Poverty
Prejudice
Respect for Life
War and Violence
Aging
Cultural and Racial Differences

American advertising often projects the image of life as Utopia. In advertisements, people are young, wealthy, and carefree. The harsh reality is that now, as in generations past, people continue to face poverty, loneliness, and death. In addition, everyone will undoubtedly experience some form of discrimination during their lifetime, if not from religion, race, or socioeconomic class, then perhaps from the universal frailty of aging.

Confronting and overcoming such problems can help a person understand society and increase his or her orientation to all of mankind. This focus is essential to improve our understanding of ourselves as individuals and in the context of society. We can learn to appreciate and enjoy differences, adding fullness to our lives. Moving beyond an egocentric frame of reference increases a person's sense of responsibility to others in need.

The ability to make moral judgments or to take moral action is developed through experience with parents and other socializing forces. The family is the primary agent of moral development, as seen in the character development of children during their preschool years. Value systems are also influenced by teachers, clergy, club leaders, and others involved with children. Interactions with others give children the opportunity to test and validate their own ideas, beliefs, and perceptions against those of others.

Peer and school experiences have a tremendous impact on children's moral development. In the peer group, boys and girls learn how to think and act; they are exposed to different values derived from a variety of families, nationalities, and socioeconomic groups. On entering school, children face even more social complexities that affect their developing values. If the school feels compelled to enhance character development, confusion may abound over what traits are important: happiness versus a sense of duty, sportsmanship versus winning, or creativity versus conformity.

Coexisting with the forces influencing children's moral development are the intellectual and emotional needs of children. Children exhibit a need for information that will help them understand the world beyond their own community. This knowledge of other people enhances their sense of belonging to a special group that has its own unique characteristics and its own place in the world.

Long before children are aware of the need to know the world beyond their home or to develop their own values, however, parents are in a position to influence children's sense of moral judgment and responsibility to others. Parents have the first opportunity to share their own values and beliefs with their children and to broaden their children's horizons so that they can better understand society.

From the earliest years of children's lives, parents and other adults in their environment can help them develop a healthy regard for all life and respect for individual freedom. As they grow, boys and girls need a chance to ask questions, to help with decision making, and to take a stand for their own beliefs. Answers from adults should be honest so that children can sort out conflicting values and understand the realities of life.

Parents and other caregivers have the opportunity to instill in children their own beliefs and values not only through words, but also through actions. In most cases, boys and girls will follow the adult's lead in their response to violence, poverty, or prejudice. Children can be further influenced through exposure to new experiences and through books.

While it may be impossible or undesirable for children to experience something firsthand, books offer a variety of situations with which children can indirectly interact to form opinions. Stories help children experience a variety of life situations and see how the characters handle crisis. Reading about different ethnic groups and various lifestyles also can affect the attitudes of children.

There is a tendency for adults to want to protect children from the cruel realities of life, but it is not possible to isolate them from bigotry, controversy, or killing. It surrounds children on television and in the papers. Books on poverty and war may not seem appropriate reading for children, but they do show another part of life beyond American affluence. Children can deal with these situations if they are shared with a caring adult. The ensuing discussion of stories thus can add significance to life.

When shared with children, books can help bridge cultural, religious, and age barriers or show the futility of war. Stories about conflicts caused by differences in socioeconomic status and ethnic background can teach children how to deal with these differences before the conflicts teach them bigotry. Books promoting respect for all life and individual needs and rights can help children understand society and develop their own value system.

Heroes and heroines of stories can provide a sense of hope as they meet poverty with courage. Other characters who suffer the adversities of prejudice, isolation, or war can stimulate serious thinking about these atrocities. Such books can facilitate discussion between children and their caregivers about their own beliefs. Stories should not be seen as a lesson, but rather as a stimulus for discussing the book, allowing children their own reactions, thoughts, and conclusions.

The books included in this chapter were selected to help children understand the more global problems surrounding them. Some of the books were included because racial differences have an impact on the story. All the books described here are relevant to the problems of mankind and represent the best books available. Unfortunately, the availability of certain titles is limited, especially those on war and poverty.

General

Antrim's Orange, Sylvia Sunderlin, Ill. by Diane De Groat, Scribner, 1976. Ages 7–10.

In World War II England, Antrim is given an orange that he decides to keep, not eat. Unfortunately, first the teacher mistakes the orange for a gift, then Antrim drops it. Sharing the orange with friends, Antrim is devastated when his piece of it is destroyed. He refuses his teacher's reserved segment, but savors the small navel.

A Little at a Time, David A. Adler, Ill. by N.M. Bodecker, Random, 1976. Ages 4 + .

A young boy questions his grandpa about change as they walk through the city to visit a museum. Grandpa patiently explains that all things, both good and bad, happen "a little at a time." The wonders of nature, pollution, savoring an experience, and learning, all occur slowly. Contains captivating illustrations. *Highly recommended.*

A New Coat for Anna, Harriet Ziefert, Ill. by Anita Lobel, Knopf, 1986. Ages 4–7.

Anna's mother promises her a new winter coat when World War II ends. However, after the war, money is scarce. Anna's mother barters her precious possessions with a farmer and craftsmen, and after a year Anna has a new coat. A beautifully illustrated tale that incorporates concepts of perseverance and patience.

Ⓡ *The Patchwork Quilt*, Valerie Flournoy, Ill. by Jerry Pinkney, Dutton, 1985. Ages 5–8.

A gentle story about a year in the life of a black family which focuses on making a patchwork quilt. Grandma and Tanya begin the quilt with scraps of clothing contributed by each family member. Grandma becomes ill, but Tanya's dedication gradually involves the entire family in completing the quilt. *Highly recommended.*

Poverty

Ⓡ *A Chair for My Mother*, Vera B. Williams, Greenwillow, 1982. Ages 5–8.

When a fire destroys their furniture, a girl, her mother, and Grandma save coins in their money jar to buy a chair. Friends and neighbors generously give them furnishings, but they have no big comfortable chair. After a year of working, scrimping, and saving, they buy their special chair. The family's reduced economic circumstances provide a realistic contrast to the typical affluent portrayal.

Ⓡ *Tight Times*, Barbara S. Hazen, Ill. by Trina S. Hyman, Viking, 1979; Penguin, 1983. Ages 5–8.

A boy's daddy explains that the family cannot have a dog because of financial difficulties. After his dad loses his job, the child brings home a scrawny kitten and is confronted by his anguished parents. The boy's explanation triggers the release of pent-up emotions and strengthens the bonding of the family.

We Be Warm Till Springtime Comes, Lillie D. Chaffin, Ill. by Lloyd Bloom, Macmillan, 1980. Ages 5–9.

The icy cold wind blows through the old Appalachian cabin Jimmy lives in with his mama and Baby Mary. He decides that if he's big enough to freeze to death, he can brave the treacherous tunnel called the coal bank. Jimmy courageously fetches coal and wood to warm the family until springtime.

Prejudice

Living in Two Worlds, Maxine B. Rosenberg, photographs by George Ancona, Lothrop, 1986. Ages 7–12.

Children from four biracial families discuss how they feel about their cultural and racial backgrounds and how these factors influence their lives. They are proud of their heritage, but prefer not to be singled out as different. An excellent nonfiction introduction intended to increase social awareness and the understanding of biracial children.

A Look at Prejudice and Understanding, Rebecca Anders, photographs by Maria S. Forrai, Lerner, 1976. Ages 5–8.

A photo-essay introducing the concepts of prejudice and understanding. Religious and racial differences are among the reasons people use to prejudge and avoid or hurt others. In contrast, those without prejudice enjoy personal growth through discovering and understanding other people and their beliefs. Recommended with reservations because of the book's simplistic approach.

(R) *Molly's Pilgrim*, Barbara Cohen, Ill. by Michael J. Deraney, Lothrop, 1983. Ages 6–9.
At school, Molly is teased about her clothes and her poor English. When Molly is assigned to make a Pilgrim doll, her mother helps but dresses it in a costume that she, a Russian Jew, wore coming to America. Molly feels humiliated until her teacher helps her classmates understand that Molly's family are modern Pilgrims. *Highly recommended.*

Respect for Life

All the Cats in the World, Sonia Levitin, Ill. by Charles Robinson, Harcourt, 1982. Ages 5–8.
The cynical lighthouse keeper taunts Mikala about the futility of feeding abandoned cats because so many in the world are hungry. But when Mikala becomes ill, the lighthouse keeper, realizing his own job of guiding ships is similar, feeds the cats for her. His action is the beginning of their friendship.

(R) *Fireflies!*, Julie Brinckloe, Macmillan, 1985. Ages 5–8.
A young boy is fascinated by fireflies and thrilled when he catches a jar full of them. Watching them from his bed, the boy compares them to moonlight. The painful experience of seeing their lights dim prompts him to free them. The book's text and illustrations capture the poignant message of respect for life.

A Thousand Pails of Water, Ronald Roy, Ill. by Vo-Dinh Mai, Knopf, 1978. Ages 6–8.
Despite his village's economic dependence on whaling, Yukio cannot understand why his father hunts whales. Discovering a beached whale, the persevering Yukio carries water to keep it wet until the tide returns. Exhausted, Yukio realizes that he cannot do it alone. With compassion, his father and the villagers help save the whale.

Thy Friend, Obadiah, Brinton Turkle, Viking, 1969; Penguin 1982. Ages 5–8.
Obadiah, a young Quaker boy, is embarrassed to have a seagull following him. When his family teases him about his new friend, he throws a stone at it. After several days, the gull returns with a fish hook caught in

its beak. Obadiah gently removes the hook and acknowledges the friendship. A classic about respect for living creatures.

War and Violence

Bang Bang You're Dead, Louise Fitzhugh and Sandra Scoppettone, Ill. by Louise Fitzhugh, Harper, 1969. Ages 5–8.

James and his friends play "bang bang, you're dead" with toy guns on the neighborhood hill. When big Mike's gang challenges their ownership, war is declared. Fighting with rocks and sticks, the boys inflict wounds. In the bloody aftermath, the boys realize the futility of war and agree to use the hill together.

Harald and the Giant Knight, Donald Carrick, Clarion, 1982. Ages 5–8.

Young Harald idolizes the Baron's knights until they take over the farmers' land. Instead of helping people as Harald envisions, the knights destroy and plunder. Harald and his parents concoct a plan that rids them of the knights and restores their land. This story provides an excellent balance to the fairytale exaltation of chivalry.

Nobody Wants a Nuclear War, Judith Vigna, Albert Whitman, 1986. Ages 6–8.

A sister and brother build a shelter to protect themselves from a nuclear war. Their mother finds them and reassures the children that while others share their fear, many people are working to prevent such devastation. By making a banner, the children express their goal for a safe world. A milestone in children's literature on this subject.

Aging

Buffy and Albert, Charlotte Pomerantz, Ill. by Yossi Abolafia, Greenwillow, 1982. Ages 5–8.

A young girl describes her grandfather and his very old cats, Buffy and Albert. Because of their unsavory habits, Grandpa considers them a nuisance. When Grandpa twists his ankle and is cared for by his family, he develops a new appreciation for his equally vulnerable cats. An interesting approach to the problems of aging.

(R) ***Emma***, Wendy Kesselman, Ill. by Barbara Cooney, Doubleday, 1980. Ages 4–8.

Emma has many children and grandchildren, but usually she is alone. Inspired by a painting she receives for her seventy-second birthday, Emma begins to paint. Her paintings of things she loves are admired by many people, but best of all they free her from her loneliness.

The Hundred Penny Box, Sharon B. Mathis, Ill. by Leo and Diane Dillon, Viking, 1975. Ages 6–10.

Great-great-Aunt Dew moves in with Michael's family. He delights in hearing her tell stories about the hundred pennies she keeps in a dilapidated old box, a penny for each of her birthdays. As Michael's mother strives to replace the big, ugly box, he protects it and realizes his love for Aunt Dew. *Highly recommended*.

I Dance in My Red Pajamas, Edith T. Hurd, Ill. by Emily A. McCully, Harper, 1982. Ages 5–8.

Jenny's parents think her grandparents are old, so they warn her not to shout or jump when she goes visiting. Jenny knows better; her grandparents love a noisy day. Together they play the whirling game, pound together a cathouse, and sing and dance. The book's illustrations capture the joyful exuberance of the threesome. *Highly recommended*.

Old Mother Witch, Carol Carrick, Ill. by Donald Carrick, Clarion, 1975. Ages 5–9.

David's friends call his neighbor, Mrs. Oliver, "Old Mother Witch," because she complains about dogs and balls in her yard. Prompted into taunting her, David discovers Mrs. Oliver lying on her porch, the victim of a heart attack. Guilty and ashamed, David receives Mrs. Oliver's shy gratitude with newfound understanding. *Highly recommended*.

Ultra-Violet Catastrophe!, Margaret Mahy, Ill. by Brian Froud, Parents Mag. Pr., 1975. O.P. Ages 5–9.

Sally doesn't want to exchange her jeans for a dress or visit fussy Aunt Anne. But there she meets Uncle Magnus, whose favorite phrase is "ultra-violet catastrophe." Crawling through hedges and wading in mud, they discover their kindred spirit. Scolded by Aunt Anne for their dishevelment, they part with promises of future visits. *Highly recommended*.

Wilfred Gordon McDonald Partridge, Mem Fox, Ill. by Julie Vivas, Kane Miller Bk., 1985. Ages 5–8.

Wilfred Gordon lives next to an old people's home. When his favorite, Miss Nancy, losses her "memory," he questions the residents about the word's meaning. Wilfred Gordon restores Miss Nancy's memory with items each resident has described. Things to make her laugh and cry, and things from long ago, each conjures a significant event.

Cultural and Racial Differences

The Bicycle Man, Allen Say, Houghton, 1982. Ages 5–8.

Sports day in occupied Japan is described by a young schoolboy.

Lunch follows the class games, then the parents and teachers run races. The villagers are fearful when two American soldiers interrupt the festivities. Smiling and bowing, the soldiers borrow a bicycle and participate in sports day. Exemplifies intercultural respect without moralizing. *Highly recommended*.

The Birthday Visitor, Yoshiko Uchida, Ill. by Charles Robinson, Scribner, 1975. Ages 5–8.

Japanese-American Emi is angry that her birthday will be spoiled by another stuffy minister from Japan. However, Rev. Okura is an unexpected surprise. He is young, performs a funeral for a bird, and takes off his shoes underneath the table. Overcoming her prejudice, Emi has a wonderful birthday celebration.

The Castle on Hester Street, Linda Heller, Jewish Pubs., 1982. Ages 6–8.

For every fabricated tale Grandfather tells his granddaughter, Julie, about coming to America from Russia, Grandmother relates the true story. Grandfather jokes about his castle, but Grandmother speaks of the hardships of Jews coming to a new land. But both grandparents agree on the blessing of living in freedom.

Cornrows, Camille Yarbrough, Ill. by Carole Byard, Coward, 1979. Ages 7–10.

Sister and her brother, Me Too, learn the history of "cornrows" as Great Grammaw and Mama fix their hair that way. They learn that although named for the rows of corn found on slave plantations, the style originated in Africa, symbolizing rank and tribe. Today it symbolizes pride in their black heritage.

Everett Anderson's Year, Lucille Clifton, Ill. by Ann Grifalconi, Holt, 1974. O.P. Ages 5–8.

Poems for each month highlight both memorable and ordinary events in Everett Anderson's life. Playing in the February snow gives Everett a chocolate nose and vanilla toes. Lack of sugar prevents him from making America's birthday cake. Everett delights in his Halloween mask and expresses his gratitude at Thanksgiving. A story with universal appeal. *Highly recommended*.

Gooseberries to Oranges, Barbara Cohen, Ill. by Beverly Brodsky, Lothrop, 1982. Ages 6–9.

Fanny, age eight, reluctantly leaves her cholera-ravaged Russian village to join her father in America. There Fanny sees squalor and poverty, despite Papa's promise of a golden land. Education and a friend await her, but Fanny doesn't feel America is home until a sweet-tasting orange replaces the memories of gooseberries in Russia.

® *How My Parents Learned to Eat*, Ina R. Friedman, Ill. by Allen Say, Houghton, 1984. Ages 5–8.

The narrator's parents never eat together during their courtship. Her father, an American sailor, is afraid to use chopsticks, and her mother, a Japanese schoolgirl, has never used a knife and fork. Secretly, each masters the other's technique of eating. Now in their own home, the family alternates styles, enjoying both cultures.

® *The Long Way to a New Land*, Joan Sandin, Harper, 1981. Ages 6–8. An I can read history book.

As Carl Erik and his family face famine in Sweden in 1868, his uncle writes, urging them to come to America. The family suffers many hardships on their boat trip to the "new land." Arriving in America, they eat wheat bread with butter, symbolic of the promise of their new life.

Related Titles

General

Poverty

Hi, Mrs. Mallory, Ianthe Thomas.

Miss Maggie, Cynthia Rylant.

So What If I'm a Sore Loser?, Barbara Williams.

Respect for Life

Do You Love Me?, Dick Gackenbach.

Aging

Annie and the Old One, Miska Miles.

Grandpa Doesn't Know It's Me, Donna Guthrie.

I Know a Lady, Charlotte Zolotow.

Magic and the Night River, Eve Bunting.

My Grandpa Retired Today, Elaine Knox-Wagner.

A Special Trade, Sally Wittman.

Cultural and Racial Differences

Amifika, Lucille Clifton. (Black)

Angel Child, Dragon Child, Michelle M. Surat. (Vietnamese)

Brother Mouky and the Falling Sun, Karen Whiteside. (Black)

Chin Chiang and the Dragon's Dance, Ian Wallace. (Chinese)

Daddy, Jeannette Caines. (Black)

Everett Anderson's Goodbye, Lucille Clifton. (Black)

First Pink Light, Eloise Greenfield. (Black)

Freddy, My Grandfather, Nola Langner. (Hungarian)

A Gift for Tia Rosa, Karen T. Taha. (Mexican American)

Grandmama's Joy, Eloise Greenfield. (Black)

The Happy Funeral, Eva Bunting. (Chinese)

Jafta's Mother, Hugh Lewin. (African)

The Legend of Scarface: A Blackfeet Indian Tale, Robert San Souci. (American Indian)

My Brother Fine with Me, Lucille Clifton. (Black)

Not Just Any Ring, Danita R. Haller. (American Indian)

Sadako and the Thousand Paper Cranes, Eleanor Coerr. (Japanese)

Wagon Wheels, Barbara Brenner. (Black)

When Grandfather Journeys into Winter, Craig K. Strete. (American Indian)

Author-Title Index

Hest, Amy, 73
Hi, Mrs. Mallory!, 102–3
Hickman, Martha W., 21, 33, 34, 59, 67–68
Hiding House, 97
Highest Balloon on the Common, 84
Hines, Anna G., 136
Hirsch, Karen, 129
His Mother's Dog, 46
Hitz, Demi, 45
Hoban, Lillian, 136
Hoban, Russell, 96
Hodges, Margaret, 82
Hogan, Bernice, 22
Hogan, Paula and Kirk Hogan, 112
Holes and Peeks, 88
Holz, Loretta, 65
Home Alone, 36
Honest Andrew, 3
Hoopes, Lyn L., 22, 50
Horrible Hannah, 8
Horwitz, Elinor, 82
Hospital Book, 112
Hospital Roadmap: A Book to Help Explain the Hospital Experience to Young Children, 112
Hospital Scares Me, 112
Hospital Story: An Open Family Book for Parents and Children Together, 112
Hound and Bear, 97
How: Making the Best of a Mistake, 6
How My Parents Learned to Eat, 149
Howe, James, 31, 87, 112
Hubbard, Kate and Evelyn Berlin, 14
Hug Me, 48
Hughes, Shirley, 31, 34, 35, 36, 87
Hundred Penny Box, 147
Hurd, Edith, 25, 147
Hurwitz, Johanna, 9, 34, 77
Hutchins, Pat, 60

I Am Adopted, 62
I Can Do It by Myself, 120–21
I Can Share, 8
I Can't Always Hear You, 126
I Can't Hear like You, 126
I Dance in My Red Pajamas, 147
I Don't Care, 31
I Don't Want to Go to School, 29
I Don't Want to Go to School Book, 29–30
I Feel: A Picture Book of Emotions, 42
I Had a Bad Dream: A Book about Nightmares, 86
I Hate Kisses, 41
I Hate My Brother Harry, 74
I Hate Red Rover, 121
I Have a Sister, My Sister Is Deaf, 126
I Have Two Families, 64

I Know a Lady, 42
I Like You to Make Jokes with Me, but I Don't Want You to Touch Me, 16
I Love You Mouse, 48
I Never Win!, 121
I Started School Today, 30
I Think He Likes Me, 74
I Want a Brother or Sister, 74
I Want That!, 6
I Wish I Had My Father, 71
I Wish I Was Sick, Too!, 106
I Wish Laura's Mommy Was My Mommy, 58
I'll Always Love You, 25
I'll Bet You Thought I Was Lost, 84
I'll Never Love Anything Ever Again, 108
I'll Tell on You, 4
I'm Coming to Get You!, 85
I'm Deaf and It's Okay, 126
I'm Moving, 33
I'm Not Moving, 33
I'm Not Oscar's Friend Anymore, 97
I'm Terrific, 121
Ichikawa, Satomi, 94
If He's My Brother, 8
If It Weren't for Benjamin (I'd Always Get to Lick the Icing Spoon), 74–75
If You Listen, 71
Ira Sleeps Over, 88
Is That Your Sister?: A True Story of Adoption, 62
Isadora, Rachel, 34–35, 138
It's Me, Claudia, 121
It's Mine!, 44
It's My Body, 14
It's Not Fair, 121
It's Not Your Fault, 16
It's Okay to Look at Jamie, 130
It's Okay to Say No!, 14
Ivan the Great, 4
Iwamura, Kazuo, 95

Jacobson, Jane, 32–33
Jafta, 41
Jafta's Father, 71
Jafta's Mother, 49
Jamie's Tiger, 126–27
Jamie's Turn, 128
Jance, Judith A., 15–16
Jane, Wishing, 121–22
Jealousy, 46
Jeffers, Susan, 10
Jeff's Hospital Book, 112
Jenny's Baby Brother, 75
Jenny's Cat, 33
Jensen, Virginia A., 40
Jewell, Nancy, 2, 23, 35

No Friends, 102
No Good in Art, 122
No Measles, No Mumps for Me, 106
No More Secrets for Me, 17
Nobody Wants a Nuclear War, 146
Nobody's Perfect, Not Even My Mother, 122
Nolan, Madeena S., 138
Nonna, 23
Not at Home, 98–99
Not Just Any Ring, 82
Now One Foot, Now the Other, 109
Numeroff, Laura J., 94, 107
Nursery School, 30

O'Brien, Anne S., 6
Octavia Told Me a Secret, 95
Oink and Pearl, 77
Old Mother Witch, 147
Oldest Kid, 60
Oliver Button Is a Sissy, 138
Oliver Hyde's Dishcloth Concert, 6
Ominsky, Elaine, 128
On My Own: The Kid's Self-Care Book 115
On the Way to the Movies, 60
Once Upon a Dinkelsbuhl, 82
One More Time, 64
Oneal, Zibby, 76
Orgel, Doris, 26, 103
Osborn, Lois, 58
Other Emily, 46
Our Teacher's in a Wheelchair, 131
Out to Sea, 115
Owly, 49
Oxenbury, Helen, 29

Palmer, Pat, 123
Parenteau, Shirley, 84
Patchwork Quilt, 144
Paterson, Diane, 10
Patrick and Ted, 99
Patrick, Yes You Can, 132
Patrick's Dinosaurs, 85–86
Patty Gets Well, 109
Peabody, 49
Pearson, Susan, 51, 58, 76, 137, 139
Peavy, Linda, 20
Peck, Richard, 86
Peet, Bill, 81
Perez, Carla and Deborah Robison, 111
Perry, Patricia and Mariette Lynch, 64
Peterson, Jeanne W., 72, 126
Petey, 26
Pfister, Marcus, 101
Philips, Barbara, 124
Phillips, Mildred, 4
Phoebe Dexter Has Harriet Peterson's Sniffles, 107

Pippin and Pod, 9
Poinsettia and Her Family, 77
Poinsettia and the Firefighters, 89
Poisons Make You Sick, 115–16
Polushkin, Maria, 7, 49
Pomerantz, Charlotte, 146
Poor Boy, Rich Boy, 62
Porcupine's Christmas Blues, 95
Porte, Barbara A., 36, 56, 108
Potters' Kitchen, 34–35
Power, Barbara, 58
Powers, Mary E., 131
Prall, Jo, 129
Prince and the Pink Blanket, 11
Princess Pearl, 77
Private Zone, 15

Quilts in the Attic, 77

Rabe, Berniece, 130
Rachel and Obadiah, 139
Rajesh, 131
Ray, Deborah K., 51
Red Lion, 82
Ride the Red Cycle, 131
Right Now, 51
Robinet, Harriette G., 131
Robins, Joan, 99
Robinson, Nancy K., 10
Robison, Deborah, 11, 87
Roche, P.K., 73
Rockwell, Anne, 139–40
Rockwell, Anne and Harlow Rockwell, 87, 107, 111, 115
Rockwell, Harlow, 30, 110, 110–11
Rogers, Fred, 29, 110, 125
Rollo and Juliet, 40
Rosen, Winifred, 74
Rosenberg, Maxine B., 123–24, 144
Rosie and Michael, 95
Ross, G. Max, 32
Ross, Pat, 98
Ross, Pat and Joel, 37
Ross, Tony, 85
Roth, Harold, 30, 110
Roy, Ron, 40, 70–71, 109, 128
Roy, Ronald, 145
Russell, Pamela and Beth Stone, 14
Russell Rides Again, 9
Rylant, Cynthia, 51, 103

Sadako and the Thousand Paper Cranes, 23
Saddest Time, 23
Safety First: Home, 116
Safety Zone: A Book Teaching Child Abduction Prevention Skills, 17
Saint George and the Dragon, 82

Subject Index

Maureen Cuddigan is branch children's librarian at the Dakota County Library in Burnsville, Minnesota.

Mary Beth Hanson is a pediatric nurse practitioner at the Park Nicollet Medical Center in St. Louis Park, Minnesota.